BONFIRE OF ROADMAPS

Brad and Michele Moore Roots Music Series

Requests for permission to reproduce mate-
rial from this work should be sent to:
Permissions
University of Texas Press
P.O. Box 7819
Austin, TX 78713-7819
http://utpress.utexas.edu/about
/book-permissions

⊗ The paper used in this book meets the
minimum requirements of ANSI/NISO
Z39.48-1992 (R1997) (Permanence of Paper).

Library of Congress Cataloging-
in-Publication Data

Ely, Joe.
Bonfire of roadmaps / Joe Ely. — 1st ed.
  p. cm. — (Brad and Michele Moore
roots music series)
ISBN 978-0-292-71653-7 (cloth : alk. paper)
  1. Ely, Joe—Travel. 2. Country musi-
cians—Travel. 3. Voyages and travels—
Poetry. 4. Lyric poetry.
I. Title.
  ML420.E54A3 2007
  782.421642092—dc22
[B]   2006023534

ISBN 978-0-292-75629-8 (pbk. : alk. paper)

doi:10.7560/716537

JOE ELY

BONFIRE of ROADMAPS

University of Texas Press ✧ Austin

CONTENTS

52 CITIES TILL CHRISTMAS

Damn, Damn, Damn I kick my self out the door
Dragging my ball and chain
The yard cats scatter and the buzzards take flight
Crazy ol' Joe is back on the road

First stop London, God not again
I haven't been there since the Gulf War made pebbles
From the proud stone banks of the Mesopotamia
And sold the rights to CNN and BBC

I take that back, I was there last week
Seeing the city through Marie's eyes of innocence
Tug boats became swans, busses, red castles on wheels
In a throng of storybook faces

And through the eyes of Sharon
Who saw the fabric, the lace and the burlap
The scarves and shawls that drape the city
And the blossoms on rusty security bars

Am I becoming another weary gypsy
Like those in Barcelona, drinking wine
At Public monuments and Urinals
Whose world has shriveled to a paper sack?

Jimmy called this morning
Worried about his father, 83 and waning
Saying sometime in the tour he might take leave
If his father's condition does worsen

We meet at the airport with huge red bags
Carter and Charles look like Irish Sherpas
Ready to make a climb to the Sunrise and back
We have 52 cities before Christmas

Back in the belly of the proverbial bird
And back to my seat at the back of the plane
Tho I'm not smoking now, I sit with the smokers
In training for the nights to follow

The man to my left looks through photographs
Of himself walking on coals, juggling fire
A drunken Detroit blonde has been cut off from the spigot
So she's conning me into rustling up her drinks

I toss and turn and shudder with reality
It'll be months till I see my girls again
Tho their smiles I carry with me
And give me strength when lights are low

We skid in to Gatwick parting the Red Fog
And take our place in the notorious queue
A mini van is waiting and we groan at the sight
As memories come back to smite us

I cash it in at the hotel and begin a deep troubled sleep
It blows me back to the dusty ol' Plains
My father came to tell me how he tried to hang on
But the forces of nature were against him

I vaguely remember my ancestors of old
Walking in the curves of Piccadilly
Ian says that England is trapped in its own history
Cruel nature doth trick the lazy to change

And change is in the wind and the News is hungry
There's trouble in the Beehive, the Royal family's pumpin'
    honey
They're feigning so cool, so wholesome, so majestic
Tho history is serving them an eviction notice with a gun to
    their head

Maybe a premonition, maybe it was in the wind
But Jimmy got a call from his sweet Claire
"Your daddy, he died at the dining room table
Across the ocean in sad Del Rio"

Poor Jimmy heads back across the Briny Drink
A half of a day into the tour
Our grief, in harmony, travels with him
As he is the soul of the band

The next day is a tempest, pre-show panic
We need a bass player who can learn the set in an instant
My whole life boiled down to a couple of hours
And the tour begins tonight in Leeds

I rush to the station with Carter and Charles
Missing our first train, catching the next
Screeching in to the station, the Irish Center by taxi
The souls of my boots still smoking

I play Leeds solo, just me and my guitar
And face culture shock, stone alone
The crowd seems not to mind that the band is vapor
And that the hotel is a Holiday Inn

Foggy Leeds floats in yellow light
And affects the brain, banana pudding
Such was explained to me by a Leeds professor
Who stood by the stage farting theories

The next morning we travel much too early
Out the top of England and in to Quixotic Scotland
Watching the landscape grow gray and green
While the cheeks of the travelers glow redder

Glasgow sings to the hard workin' man
I suppose we qualify, this ol' road ain't easy
Andy has just flown in to learn Jimmy's parts
With a two hour rehearsal at the Rock Garage

Glasgow smokes, we play with a passion
The bass is right in the pocket
I can rest a little easier, the band can go on
As we bid Sweet Scotland a Texas goodnight

An old stuffed Polar Bear 'neath a dusty Chandelier
Greets us at the hotel in Manchester
Flanked by Tigers and Snow Owls in a gross display
Of the Art of Mad Dogs and Englishmen

I'm reminded at the show of the old Armadillo
Falling into space from the 8-foot stage

Singing to the vacuum inside of a deep emptiness
Wishing for my mother's womb

Cows in the soccer field, sheep on the golf course
Sheffield was a pleasure to play
With pretty girls on the front row smiling to the beat
And after the show they invite you to tea

The cemetery in Sheffield is one of the best I've ever seen
But I wouldn't want to be buried there
The steel mills of Sheffield are much too close
And the gates are wet and rusting

The outer forest of the land of Nottingham
Has long been stripped and paved with Population
A large percentage prefer New Fairy over Old Fairy
To keep their China sparkling White

A day off in Cambridge and a Laundromat nearby
I walk the town Lost in Time
I feel I've been here, centuries in the mist
I add it to my list of Déjá Vu's

On stage at Cambridge the lights were green
There was a wall between the crowd and the band
First it was cellophane, then glass, then ceramic, then rock
Sometimes you're Backslapped, sometimes Snake bit

I attempt to act natural when the show is over
I go out to meet faces from the Future Past
It was good to see Gay from the Cambridge Folk Fest
With the music she shared so naturally

We drive East to Ely with the bells at noon
Through the manicured fields of Anglia

I search for signs of ancestral memory
But come up with a "possible maybe"

The Isle of Ely was just a bump in the bog
Until Etheldreda built a hangout for wayward monks
But the Danes kept raiding and the Picts kept barkin'
The Saxons didn't get much sleep

Never have I seen a more amazing cathedral
With a central tower in the shape of an octagon
The sermon in progress met an untimely end
When feedback howled from the church P.A.

The priest put the blame on the microphone switch
This was a very kind thing to do
But our presence, I felt, was the source of it all
When this loud band entered the sanctimonious silence

Post Tempestata Tranquillita Deluxe
Descended upon me as I opened my heart
To the glow of stained glass and organ music
And the visual magnificence of the Preserved Past

What in our world will be thus preserved?
The graceful architecture of freeway intersections?
Long after automobiles have served their usefulness
Will the Golden Gate and Brooklyn Bridge survive?

Surely not the steel brick cubes that scar the modern city
Built from the Greed of Monster Companies
What will survive from Pop, Rap, Punk, Rave, Metal or
    Country?
Nothing will survive so what price vanity??

Shepherd's pie on a shingle was served in the pub
And either cod or plaice dressed with chips
Not much has happened between 1181 and 1992
That cannot be explained by ghosts

Damn, Damn, Damn we're floundering out here
And everyone blames everyone else
Maybe it's time that I get arrested for scandals
Or spit blood on stage for publicity

There's a crack in the road just starting to form
Between the records and the right of way
Clouds are forming in my hotel rooms
And lightning flies out of my ass

Carter and Charles bring nothing but bad news
From agents, managers, promoters,
Any dickhead in their path with an opinion
Over and over, it's weighing me down

I lost the early band to rumors and hearsay
Spread by the road crew, Bo and Hatch
Gossip crawled through their eyes like maggots
Until Mutiny became an Exit to Freedom

I felt my brain enter another reality
Disconnected to the matter that clutters the earth
I walk on stage at Norwich all alone and begin to play
A song I didn't know and don't know why I played

The faces in the crowd all seemed familiar
I imagined they were all in my computer
The light man lit me with a yellow X
Each song pierced me with a sword

I somehow made it back to this world
The rumble of the music shook me out of the dark
The next morning I climbed back aboard the van
Like some Hillbilly Hunchback of Notre Dame

The Boars Head in Fareham rose from a field
We got a feeling we were close to heaven

All the poisons from the night before I left on stage
At sound check and scattered through the parking lot

I've played out my life in hotel rooms
Two tables, a chair, a bed, a TV
My imagination has kept me company
The four walls play back pictures from my painted past

I need to watch more TV
I'm feeling like I don't exist anymore
TV makes one feel connected and insignificant
TV, TV take me in your arms, make love to me

I see Lady Chatterley in the drugstore
Buying gauze to wrap her chandelier in
Her crippled husband sits at home in the bathtub
Knowing fool well she'll go to the honky tonk tonight

God I miss the desert
Riding in this clammy, airless, smoke-trap
I miss the windows down, bugs on the windshield
Space and sky reflected in the spinning chrome wheel

You don't just drive into London, you pry into it
Like a maze, you peel away layer after layer
Over bridges, through gates, the city absorbs you
And stirs you in the human cauldron

Remembering back to the Towne and Country
Great high ceilings and a stage of Wood
We could've done sound check for hours if not
For Mary Costello's Radio Show

London is the greatest collection of eccentrics in the world
Collecting any thing on the planet that's collectable
Tangible or Intangible, Material or intellectual
And they stuff it in the cracks around London Town

After the show, the backstage became an aquarium
As Wonderful Souls from the Past came floating by
As if in a newsreel, sepia-toned and scratched
Will there be any Hoboes in Heaven?

Just about the time somebody steals the Wine
I hear there's a Snooker Hall open All Night
After a Trendy, Stuffy party we go singing
Red Ball, Number Ball, Taxi take us one and all

We play until the balls leave colored trails
Then we cab it back to the Rock and Roll Hotel
The bar is open and Ian has lost his shirt
To some beautiful but pissed-off table of debutantes

The Kings Hotel in Newport, Wales
Is a Fantasy Island of Rock and Roll
Bo Diddley piped in the Red Carpet Lobby
And Chandeliers full of Potatoes and Meat

We play our hearts out and the Welsh give a cheer
We raise our cups and return the toast
Later that night we watched the Presidential Debate
Live on TV from our bizarre country over the sea

We crawl, groaning into the bus at 2 A.M.
In order to reach the London airport by daylight
I realize I've left my red silk shirt at the Kings Hotel
What the hell, red is the color Sir Richard was buried in

I was pinned to the wall on the long flight home
I thought about the early sailors, poor bastards
Who huddled in cold, damp sailing ships
Crossing the wild Atlantic on nothing but a prayer

I could see the vast ocean curving all around me
Like a vision in a glass-covered dome

I could see the Future of the Planet of Apes
Ablaze with Bronze flesh and energized silicon

I could see the secret Governments
Hidden in black cubes the size of telephones
I could see in people's houses with walls full of water
Growing miniature vegetables in their closets

I could see vast deserts take bloom in the night
With rows of breathing mirrors aimed at satellites
Plastic houses built along unused freeways
And helicopter androids chattering to each other

I woke to a gay black steward passing out coffee
And Peyote button–looking sweet rolls
A voice in my head said what the pilot was about to say
As the pressure in my ears made my eyes swim

The English applauded when we landed in Boston
It reminded me of how proud America once was
Before the Chasm was Chiseled by Politics and Rejection
That carved a wall and moat between Cultures and the Mall

It's more visible in the East than in the West
Where greed and time have left monuments
To hollow-eyed buildings with toothless mouths
That beg you for change as you scurry past

We hover for two days in the New World
As sanity slowly recedes back to its source
The show in Boston was opened by Bristolettes
Who sing and smile like Lone Star girls

On to Portland on our new Highway ship
Bunks for all and a coffee maker
Giving us a buffer from the rigors of the highway
Not to mention costing us an eyeball and asshole

Our tight budget has got the band strapped
Making me feel alone and surrounded
By show time I short out and lose all focus
The show fell apart down a row of dominos

I finally cracked in a Portland basement
While the crowd beat on tables upstairs wanting more
And I spilled out all that was chasing me
Once and for all, not ever again

The band came alive in quaint Northampton
And charged the audience like a young bull
But instead of getting out of the way and screaming for mercy
They swooned to the danger and surrendered

New Haven sucked, plain and simple
The streets around Yale felt dangerous and wounded
As if a battle had been fought there for years on end
Mamoun's Falafel Shop was our only light

Sailing over the Susquehanna, fleeing from the North
Throws my memory nostalgic knuckle balls
Remembering the smell of the Mississippi
From a boxcar door in a Louisiana sunset

Interview after interview I spill the beans
Telling a rambling story to people who could care less
Lately I've taken to making up parts
Just to keep the plot from going stale

We played in a barn outside of DC
Financed by the big Dicks of the Corporate World
Barbara Bush was at the head of the list
But neither her nor Millie dared show their face

I went with friends to Champion Billiards
A radiant all night Pool Hall downtown somewhere
I shot 5 brilliant games and 5 that were disgraceful
And lost a hundred dollar bill just to prove it

I got in at six and the bus left at seven
The New Jersey Turnpike was ripe with whitecaps
And the bus tossed me round like a Niagara match stick
As I fondled nightmares on the couch in the back

Sharon appeared like an angel in Manhattan
And fixed me tea and massaged my road bones
In an instant all things were set right with the world
And I saw a break in the clouds in the caverns of Broadway

I felt the wind blow in from the Plains
And heard the swish of leaves from distant Chinese Elms
Her warmness like the Amarillo sun
Breaking through the Clouds above the Bowery

The commuter train to Philly is packed like a cattle car
"Make way people, there's other people need to get on."
We waited for an hour at the Ardmore station
Never suspecting the Gig was only a block away.

I played pool with DeLuka at So. Philly Billiards
And won back the money I'd lost months before
My game is taking on its own personality
It's the perfect sport for a man on the road

We make the long, long drive to Buffalo NY
In a triple-ought, ten gauge void
I don't recall a single event that took place
Suspended in road hawg amnesia

Hennessee the Niagara Mohawk
Smells his Mama's Mentholatum

Every time he's threatened by his Boss
Today he quit his job and moved in with the boss's sister

I saw him at the gig last night
Fresh in from Wilmington, with a 10,000 Maniacs T-Shirt
He left his lights on in the parking lot
And had to borrow Jumper Cables from a dentist

Maybe it's the long cold winter
But Buffalo is about as strange as they come
To the eyes of a man who comes from the desert
It's an out and out insane asylum

The gig went well, the locals came in droves
And made us feel like welcome Inmates
The stage had gremlins, a low C and a wispy treble
I blew it off and signed the ceiling at the end of the night

The expectation of crossing the border
Has the band and crew in great spirits
Singing past blues like spilling salt of difficulties Past
"No sweat today boys," says Rudy of the Road

We danced off the bus into Immigration
Into the Institution-Green-Colored-Walls waiting room
"Sorry, fools, our welcome committee says, 'your Papers ain't
    here,'
Back to beautiful Buffalo you Go."

We figured that Canada can afford to be cocky
The Blue Jays won the world series
We drive to the Concrete Falls at Niagara
Spellbound by water freefalling in a dance to gravity

The next day, Canadian election day, we're turned away again
This time the Buffalo Whirlpool nearly pulled us under
Carter is sick over loss of Toronto free time
We return head down to the Lenox Hotel

I was visited by an apparition
That swam around my room in a waltz
Liberation comes in the unlikeliest places
When the spirit soars, the senses dance

For three consecutive days we stormed the border
We call every bureaucrat we know
I put on my purple suit, shades, big boots and chest out
Like a soul singer running for President.

The papers are ready! We give a silent shout.
So long America for 18 hours
The guards want autographs and backstage passes
Not knowing us from the Prince of Wales, Ha!

The next string of cities went by in the night
Chicago, Cincinnati, Chicago again, Minneapolis, Kansas City

The gigs are getting wilder as our nerve ends spark
The coyote is driven by the moon

Michael brought me the news in a Chicago Laundromat
Ian's mother had just died in Austin
Years she had battled cancer and knowing the score
Had made peace with her loved ones long ago

Ian is far wiser than his 24 years
He explains why he's not going to the wake
His mother won't be cremated until the spring
He says they'll both be happier if he's out playing guitar

Damn, Damn, Damn, Ol' Death is a Buzzard
That swoops down upon us from time to time
I remember in my life over a seven-year period
All my family vanished in the West Texas Wind

Won't be long now till I fight away those Bastards
Picking at my flesh and plugging it with maggots
Fortunately I believe our spirits will transcend Earthy Mud
Sailing around the Stars on a Paper Airplane

Chicago has an essence that's hard to define
She's strong, she's sexy, she's addicted to power
And she protects her flock with a passion
She's a big Mother Goose with the heart of a Lion

A large part of my life is spent under hot stage lights
Moving mood to mood, reliving my life in song
Looking out in the smoky ether, looking for your face
Finding only mist and steam and dream

What bliss when the guitars spin their mean dance
Around the pounding bass as the lights change
Relentless with blasting snare and ticking hi-hat
Sanctified by the Organ aspiring to the Heavens

What bliss when there is a pool room next door
And after the show the crack of the rack
Lets all anxieties be sunk with the spheres
Into each of the six pockets of Cincinnati

Halloween back in Chicago, I go as Albert King
Ian goes as me, wearing purple suits, looking sharp
See the smiling faces, happy just to be alive
Bill and Kate and all the rest, here home away from home

We pack up to drive, give our hotel to friends
We tease the girl who came as the Queen of Bondage
Rudy drives thru the night, Noon in Minneapolis
Lunch like kings at the Club, eating to a Gospel Revue

The blue snows are beginning to swirl
Hurricane-like behind the Mother-ship
We slice through the curtain, through shards of white
While the band sloshes beer on the astro-carpet

The Phantoms of the bus are visiting me in sleep
All the other gypsies who have traveled this road
The shadows of the Fugitive fly through my dreams
As the dust does settle with the dawn

And then God made Kansas and Missouri
Cattle came up from the South, trains from the East
Yellow Wind from the West and Blue wind from the North
And wrapped it up in a barbed-wire fence

We had no trouble getting In
Amazing Grace sent down Bar-B-Q from the Heavens
It was getting Out that was tough
I could have stayed for weeks, well, maybe one more day

But no, our Itinerary precedes us
In-facked it downright slave-drives us
Handed down this sentence by a drunken jury
Who from slaves' teeth, line their pockets with gold fillings

Across the Infinite Plains, snow flakes falling
Rolling Horizon on a sea of gold
We ate in a diner with waitresses like grandmothers
Who baked pies like the Prairie, all covered in Meringue

Davis is addicted to Election 92
And I must admit the cast of characters is colorful
But Davis understands politics more than anyone
He even takes a $20 bet from me and Charles

We can barely see the TV, there's a snowstorm comin' in
Clinton is ahead we think we heard
Everyone raised their hands to simulate antennae
Yes, he's President! We let out a cheer!

Good riddance to 12 years of Republican Bullshit
Full of Phony Preachers with Phony Morals
Flooding Fistfuls of Phony Banks with Phony Money
While the Poor get poorer and Minorities get guns.

The Black Ice gets worse the closer we are to Denver
We're crawling along at twenty, sometimes fifteen
Trucks by the wayside hijacked in snow ditches lit
By red and blue lights of the Highway Patrol

Now we drag in to the Ramada E. Colfax
Head-Cold, Winged-out, Done-in and Road-Sucked

The desk clerk warned us, then warned us again—Crack
  Houses!
  Gay Bars!
Bad Dudes! Pickpockets! Working Girls! Chinese Gangs!

Mile high city of the Restless Romantic
Imaginary Vortex sung by Kerouac, Ginsburg, Neal and Corso
Visionary prophets, poets, pilgrims and potheads who either
  rose
On a cloud of incense or spilled with the wine into the gutter

City of the Plains who so believed in Induced Utopia
That they staked their very organs on that notion
Who saw their beards turn gray and their wombs turn to seed
Collecting Crystal and floating on Rocky Mt. Alpha Waves.

Dammit, Dammit, Dammit! America, I do believe
Is starting to look like the Middle Ages
Wild animals roam the jungle streets
Sick and hungry, abused, desperate, armed and blind

I see Tattoos of Tears on Children of the Streets
What once was a Latino estimate of Jail Time
Has now become a symbol of Youthful desolation
Society must share the blame and pay thru the nose

Headlines scream TROOPER SHOT!
But Greg seems to be doing just fine
Night after night walking bravely in front of beer guzzling
  crowds
Laying his stories on the line, not batting an eye

Ft. Collins was the opposite of a fortified fort
Rather an outpost on an isolated plain
They fed us well and we played all right
But I wouldn't want to die there

Glenwood Springs comes boiling out of the Mountains
Like the people on a Saturday Night
They don't cry "uncle" till the early morning light
That's the fire in Glenwood Springs

There's only a blink between oppression and freedom
And it becomes quite apparent in music
When folk meets rock for a radio-taping
Everyone walks away in a sling

The Radio Demons from the night before
Hijacked my last night of unrolling motelsleep
Tomorrow we go a thousand miles to Tucson
Following the wild Rockies tumbling into Mexico

Jimmy sheepishly approaches me
Eyes full of confession
He wrecked his motel room in a fit of frustration
Something's been bothering him it's plain to see

The road goes on forever, in a circle it seems
While he was in Del Rio buryin' his father, he conceived a
    child
Now that Claire's pregnant the circle be unbroken
And Jimmy's flippin' out at the Irony of it all

I slept hard going from Denver South
Face smashed into the bobbing couch
I looked out the window as if I had been beckoned
And saw Trinidad Mountain like in a Milosevich painting

The full moon rises over the New Mexico plain
As the twinkling lights of Santa Fe sprinkle the distance
Maria's green chili combo plate calls us
To celebrate halfway Vortex of Figure 8 Tour

A poker game begins right after passing the State Prison
And by Albuquerque the juices and quarters are flowing
Some Bet, some Pass, some Flush, some Bluff
As the Desert Moon Wafts across the Navajo Night

In Tucson, shy Confederates greet us
Who want to Verify stories they've heard
I say yes, yes it's all true; yes, we did that too
Anything you want to believe is your God-given Right

As for me, I'll believe it when I see it
And I ain't seen nothin' yet
Just give me a ten minute Sleep and a rolled-up Tortilla
And I'm one Happy Son-of-a-Bitch

Bang, Bang the show went off like a Firecracker
Rather like a Jumbo string of Black Cats
It was only Luck and an Ice-Fight at the hotel
That kept us all from waking up under a bridge in Nogales

In Phoenix the crowd stood back
And looked upon us with suspicion
That is, until I turned myself inside out
And served my still-beating heart on a Styrofoam platter

Afterwards I gravitated to the pool table
Where I showed off my skill and insincerity
By making impossible shots, winning money
And giving it all back at closing time

Into the vast thankless Void I'm so thankful for
We Plunge into the Dirty Copper Sunset
A hundred miles out the City of Angels shudders
As we cross over the Earthquake Borderline

In Southern California I hear this gnawing sound
Like a rat that's been cemented in a courthouse wall

With a squeal of Desperation
He paces like a Prisoner Doomed On Death Row

I've been worried about Michael since day one
Big City forces can gang up on a poor Texas boy
Everyone is shorting out and making mistakes
Assuming the danger of the darkness is illusion

Five guys in a New-Gold-Mercedes jump Michael
To rob him of his 12 pack of Bud
They break a bottle over his head and gash his eye
Kick him in the chest and pull out a fist full of scalp

Here we are in California the Free
And a gang of rich kids proves their manhood
By jumping a 130 lb. hippie, I'm not lying
And then gloat over their spoils in the parking lot

I'm in bed when all this goes down
When Davis calls room to room for reinforcements
They're askin' us if we wanna get it on
Leaning on their New-Gold-Mercedes

The cops approach one from each end
Hands on pistols and flashlights burning
And order everyone to take hands from pockets,
Behind their heads, spread their legs and shut up.

They search us and separate us for Questioning
These South LA cops don't take no shit
One of the assaulters tells the cops he makes fifty thousand a
    year
The Cops Handcuff him and throw him down on his hood

Off to jail they go, I feel sorry they were so dumb
We carry Michael upstairs and clean his wounds
He's weak and tired, it's 4 A.M.
And so we turn it in after a long, long day . . .

By 7 A.M. Michael's feeling worse
Him and me go in search of Emergency Rooms
Deeper into the darkness the streets feel possessed
By gangs of roving Oppressors

After two dead ends we find a hospital
Michael checks in and I wait in the lobby
Every 10 minutes Gang Members come in bleeding
Cut, shot, hit, beat, gashed, choked and broke

What has happened to you my People
The people that I love and believe in?
What vast fears do you harbor that make you destroy
The very flesh and blood that could fulfill you?

Why do you hate what you don't Understand?
Why do you escape what you need to confront?
Why is your spirit so desperate as to think
That life is so Cheap And Dispensable?

Where are you my people, where goes your soul?
Why do you travel a road that's not there?
Do you think you will find some yellow brick road
From South Central LA to the Wizard of Was?

From Long Beach south to Orange
California begins to Parody itself
Making fun of it's own Shopping Malls and Car Dealers
By constructing even bigger Shopping Malls and Car Dealers

The Swallows quit coming back to Capistrano
When the Mad Mission's Organist's fingernails quit clickin' on
    his Piano
Besides, they were tired of following perpetual traffic jams
To thousands of Taco Bells imitating Spanish Missions

Me and Ian drive our Red Rent-a-Turd
In a sudden palm-tree-sucking fog back to Long Beach
Oil refineries looked like NASA launching pads
We felt our way home through the Gauze

O City of Angels, another pilgrimage I make
O Model City of racial co-existence, what say you now?
Big Rich and Flat-Assed Poor can co-exist, what say you now?
My heart is shattered, for once I loved you, now in Vain?

I loved your Wild Surf, Your Wild Music And Style
I loved your Tans, your Blondes, your Eternal Summers
I drank wine from your Drums and smoked your Wild Sunset
And woke on your Sands to flutes and drummers

I sold you my innocence and got guilt in return
The world waits for your films that profit from death
Your people have caved in to Lechery & License
The "I deserve it" crowd believes, as Gospel, your Trick
    Advertisements

"Keep her head up Rudy she's headed for water!"
The bus weaves down the San Diego F-Way back to LA
Inside George Jones tortured us all
And reduced us to ashes by morning

I'm standin' on my head Singin' "Why, baby, Why?"
The tears keep on a fallin' "From a Window Up Above"
"The Race is On" and the poor man's a loser
"One Drink, Just One More, And Then Another"

The Roxy was tempestuous with street clothes and movie
    faces
I thought Ventura was in Texas reading poetry
Instead he shows up and gives me his latest volume:
Sitting on Moving Steel. yep, I know how you feel . . .

Ian reminds me of myself when I was his age
Quiet, Mischievous, Opinionated, and Horny
Always looking for that Perfect Place
On the edge of Trouble while remaining Perfectly Free

Later I follow Barry and Andy next door
To the Tarnished Super-Sheik joint next door
Then on to Beverly Hills next door to Elvis's
Where I sing in a den full of African Animal Faces

Adios Vatos, away we go
Wheee, wheee, outrunning the angels
Over the gap where the Earthquake sleeps
And out into the desert that winds like a snake on its belly

North to the Beautiful Brittle City by Alcatraz Bay
Where dreamers play autoharps on self-induced Clouds
Where Poets drink Espresso with Young Professionals
And charm the braziers away from their women

When the band kicked in gear I saw multicolored faces
Including the devilish grins of Terry and Jo Harvey
Must have sent my imagination reeling
For later I dreamed a harem engulfed me in ecstasy

I woke to a throbbing in my throat
I answered the phone but no words came out
I have a chill in my muscles
And another city to play to tonight

I miss Santa Clara sound check, my throat is gone
But drive to a university radio station
Safe in the library of recorded sound I sink
Up to my neck in Whos and Whens

There's no telling what Silicon Valley is up to these days
High tech spies are on the loose
Corporations like SynOptic and GenTek cast smoke screens
The New World Order will be Soft not Hard

We drive to Davis the morning after
I've reached a new physical low for this tour
At Sound Check I can't finish a single song
And Showtime is just hours away

The mind will go digging for shards of resources
When confronted with potentially hazardous situations
As my throat wouldn't let my songs cut loose
My mind remembered myths in myriad detail

The next thing I know, I had made it through
With only a few cuts and bruises
The Ego, like a Doberman on a Chain, goes looking for praise
Wagging its tail with a vengeance

The Big Drive is upon us, we shudder and gulp
Mount Shasta looms god-like a hundred miles away
The bus breaks into chatter, disconnected conversations
North to British Canada, like soldiers we march

Jimmy says that mining gold in the new world
Was what made for vast changes in trade
Instead of trading two turnips for a trout
People paid in gold and the IRS was born

Of course bartering will make a comeback in the very near
    future
When quiet fools realize that they have been taken for a ride
Living their lives around an Unnatural Ideal
Promised to them by Masters of Profit

Past Portland, Past Seattle, we drive through the night
And reach the border at 4 A.M.
Out of the Mothership and in to Immigration
Into fluorescent lights and humorless Agents

Three other busses pull up outside
The door flies back and flocks of musicians file in
Ian MacLagen from Dublin, Johnny Lee Schell from Muleshoe
Starbuck and the crew from the Rolling Stones

Woody and his wife come in half asleep
We reminisce about the last time we saw each other
Hurricane Gloria, New York City, 86
Sandbagged in his basement, with Keith and Bobby Keys . . .

Immigration became a backstage of sorts
As players from Africa and Chicago filed in
We laughed and danced and compared quick notes
Then parted just as quickly in the Canadian Night . . .

My body was a rock pile scattered with gravel
I wrestled with sleep as a last resort

I fell in her bosom just as we entered
The belly of the ferry to Victoria Bay

The diesel engine shut down and the generator died
I intended to go topside for coffee and the view
But the quiet was so strange, in its net I was caught
And rocked like a baby to the landing

I could have stayed in Victoria longer, much longer
The sun shone down and the gig went well
A pool room was open all around the clock
The hotel waited up to unlock the door

The good weather stayed and the sailing was smooth
Back on the ferry to Vancouver
The coffee was hot, the mountains were white
I healed in the goodness of the day

I remember shooting "My Baby Thinks She's French" here
    years back
And some one added words, much to my dismay
The TV crews caught me much off guard
Interviews from now till sound check

I'd forgotten what a dungeon the backstage was
In fact it had gotten worse if that were earthly possible
We gagged from the smell, like a rotten refinery
Which had left buckets of brew to turn black

Another night, who knows, they're all blurring together
So far from dear Texas, Sharon and Sweet Marie
We eat Enchilada Interpretations with cole slaw and Sorta
    Salsa
Only later did we realize this was our Thanksgiving dinner

Only four more to play, we realize in Seattle
Only two thousand miles and we'll be home

We can tell all our stories no one will believe
And then shut up and start over again

32,000 miles in 75 days,
We are the Kings of all Sailors for a while

The stage at the Backstage was warm and light
I basked in the spotlight never wanting it to end
When Reese played his solos I could listen forever
I feel an urge to be reborn as a Hammond B3

Jacob Dylan is opening the show
I can tell he's nervous, he's lookin' at his shoes
I remember how I felt when I was his age
My advice is, "Turn it up, and don't look back!"

The Place treated us great, Gregg and the Girls
And cooked Tex Mex as good as the best that there is
We hated to leave this haven of sanctuary
If only time could be more tolerant

Free spirits are those who make their own way
At the risk of being somewhat un-modern
The Snigglers in Portland are some of the finest around
They reached out for the Music so naturally

We sleep late on purpose at the Freeway Motel
And scrounge for a Cafe before we hit the road
I dress for the occasion in my Purple Sunday Suit
We're on our final leg, we're homeward bound

The Columbia River Valley is Majestic and Wild
I know it from songs Woody Guthrie once sang
The dams that gave power to the people who worked
On the Dams who used water for the power to pay

Like a moon colony in a crater
Windover, Nevada is as barren as they come
Barren in the flesh, sitting on the edge of the Dead Salt Lake
Barren in the spirit, and promising Barren Immortality

The hotel is like a Camp for the Dead
Long hallways to Nowhere, Doors seething Danger
I walked next door to the Red Garter Casino
Through the zero degree air and wind getting colder

Rows of flashing lights, digital bandits
Lit up with a promise, a chance, a peek
Computer after Computer, Programmed by Corporations
And when someone wins the bells flash, WINNER!

The Ego is justified, if only for a blink
I don't buy it for a minute, my ego wants eggs
The Casino Cafe is a Harbor for the Wasted
Gimme a Desperado Special, waitress, and a gallon of coffee

I shot pool in the Bowling alley, the green felt, inviting
The Lanes were gone, not even Bowler's Ghosts remained
And the tables all slanted this way and that
We burned a roll of quarters, me and Ian, in no time

A prostitute flashed me with a wink
As I was shooting the Eight Ball in the side
As I'd seen it before and I knew the shot
I finished the game unscathed and intact.

Later the Locals came in after work
Looking sunken-eyed, cynical and unfulfilled
Just plain people who left in search of their lives
Now their lives, in a desolate outpost, searched back for them

I wondered if I had not been so stubborn
And followed my muses from alley cat to Fool

I wondered if I might have taken a job on this moonscape
Dealing Blackjack, Slicing Onions and Fishing for Dupes

No one cries when we leave sad tragic Windover
All eyes fall to the Great Salt Desert
A Bankrupt Landscape if there ever was one
Torturing the earth with death and oblivion

My throat, gone again, this time laryngitis
I'm a sure-fire goner, empty as the West
Payless Drug fills a phoned-in prescription
And we Cancel the Gig for the first time in years

I hate to miss my very own party
But there really ain't much I could do
The Idea of a concert by telepathic transmission
Is a great idea if it weren't for the cover

Ghost lights flash around the inside of the bus
The Curtains do glow in quick colored patterns
The engine vibrates my skull, my bones
Strange Inertias toss my body like a bobbing bottle

I can make out the stars through the ice on the windows
As we inch across the Big West, Utah, Wyoming
Tetracycline and Cortisone start crawling through my body
My bones feeling brittle as the frozen brush

At the intersection in Denver the Vortex is crossed
Like Infinity on the Home Stretch with a bandaged leg
This Figure 8 is sniffing like a bloodhound
I fall asleep in the Trinidad Shadows

When the engine shuts down I know we've arrived
Santa Fe glows golden in the morning light
I'm in the DMZ between sleep and Santa Claus
Huevos Rancheros con Chile Verde is my last pure hope

I walk the old streets between Cerrillos and the Santa Fe
    Station
Remembering, as a child, dirt streets and Ponderosa smoke
Santa Fe was a warrior then, rich in tradition
Wishing that tomorrow would leave it alone

But tomorrow came and paved the roads
And Hotels built lobbies over Navajo bones
And Galleries were built with Yankee dinero
And the locals moved out to the mobile-home suburbs

The Hall was a cave, full of last week's echoes
I find Charles Ray at sound check slaying Sound Sucking
    Dragons

With every city comes a new slew of Knights
And a new Castle Keeper with a Phone and a Sword

Swimming in a vat of Self-made Feedback
Like a drunken swan in a tar pit
I curl my lips as if to blow out the candle
And scream a primordial scream instead

Thru the honky-tonk mist I see visions of my friends
Jamie, Wally, Paul and Terry floating in colored light
Amigos from Albuquerque, Gary, Palscé and Simoneaux
Indian painters and dancers, Welders and Waitresses

When the party's roaring we start our engines
And wave goodbye to the Land of Enchantment
A blizzard is approaching from the Mouth of the North
And the Lone Star State is singing our Song

South we go, across the Starry High Desert
CrisXcrossing the trails of Coronado and De Vaca
Flyin like a Roadrunner with a cold front approaching
The whole band swaying like the Happy Hearts Club

One by one the lights went out
One by one the towns flew by
We stopped for food and fuel in Way Out Ozona
Watching tumbleweeds with our coffee and toast

The weather, still cold, turned to mist and to drizzle
As the Hill Country turned in to Austin City Limits
In our hearts we'd expected the most glorious of sunsets
Instead of cold and dark when we whoa and dismount

No fanfare no trumpets, no brass band or confetti
Just a sign that said "Welcome home Shove and Anger
    Survivors"

But how beautiful to be home in mostly one piece
And the beautiful faces of the ones we love

I walked into La Zona Rosa and scarfed chips and salsa
Bouncing Marie on my lap and my arm around Sharon
Proud like a soldier home from war
Until someone at the next table said

"Oh, you been gone, I didn't know you'd even left . . ."
"What a life you have just singing and playing"
"People buying you drinks and feeding you steak"
"With big bosomed women licking your ear"

I scowled at first but then I laughed
And then I laughed some more a deep raspy laugh
And I glared at this imbecile and laughed with a vengeance
He up and left the room for no apparent reason

Maybe I just needed to laugh a little
After all the highway never hears you laugh
It just lays there beckoning the traveler with promises
And teases the gypsies with the swishing of wind

Let 'em go, foolish dreamers, let 'em follow their folly
The seven golden cities are out there, I saw each and every one
Glittering in the sunset, as I passed each one by
I have no use for cities of gold

Looking back, it's like another road dream
I was born on a roll and I'll ride till I die
Gypsies have a name for those who return
'Defenders of the Hallowed Circles'

I once dreamed I rode the Pecos with Lilly Langtry
On a Dirt-bike Harley with dual rifle scabbards
I gunned Roy Bean down in front of his PissAnt courthouse
And married Lilly in Lubbock at the First Baptist Church

And that's the way it is with Dreamers
They feel the Doom but stay one Storm ahead
If a man knows not his next destination
Then any road he takes will get him there on time

Farewell ol' highway, you've fooled me again
No Pot of Gold at the finish, just a ragged old Rainbow
And some beat-up old dreamers, huddling in the rain
Man, a hot cup of Coffee would sure be good . . .

LOVE AND DANGER TOUR
September to December 1992

IRON RHINOS

A cup of Coffee is a shortcut for a poor man's conception
A catalyst to inspire visions of a shining Silver City
Lighting up the eyes of desperado Vagabonds
Sending them reeling like fools to ludicrous destinations

From a back booth at the International House of Pancakes
I sat over coffee with Eddie "Laredo" Beethoven
Conceiving a journey of 4000 miles
With 2 guitars, 2 sleeping bags and a green tow sack between us

It was there we decided come hell or high water
To venture forth North from Lubbock in mid-October
Tossing better judgment to the wind
To see the leaves change in New England.

Peach and Judy gave us the jump-start
With a ride in Peach's weed-green Caddy
From the Hub-City Mecca to the rail yards of Amarillo
Full of pancakes and Coffee and Horizons in our eyes

We leave friends and family with a sigh of relief
And breathe deeply as Fort Lubbock sinks in the mirror

We crank up Spanish Radio "Eat my Burrito" and sing along
   with glee
As the cotton fields of Plainview go whispering by

I Recall an earlier journey from my Euro-troubadour days
When a wild-eyed Parisian archeologist
Brought a key to the ancient Parisian Catacombs
He'd stolen from the coffers at the Cité Université

I Tell the Catacombs story thru Tulia and Kress
Pausing only to glance at the old well and Elm tree
That still stood on the land where my father
Walked away from the dust bowl to meet a self-made fate

Laredo recalls the story of Cadillac Mountain, New England
The first spot in the U.S.A. touched by the rising sun
A Spiritual mountain among ancient tribes
Confiscated by the government in the name of
   Communication

By the town of Happy we are howling
Partly with abandon, partly with anticipation
Any new adventure brings the senses in touch
With the mysteries of the invisible

When you leave the familiar
And cross the line to everywhere else
Your soul leaps to a higher plane and gives your body
A free ride without so much as a ticket or hand stamp

And so we jump from the cushy leather seats of a Cadillac
To the old Rock Island rail yards of my Childhood
Where my grandfather landed on his Lifetime journey
When he left familiar Arkansas for the promise of the West

And there he stayed for fifty years
He raised a family and built a house

Where my mother was born to the sound of Iron Rhinos
And where I was born to the same monster roar

We see a Brakeman in the late afternoon sun
With railroad eyes and crow's feet like the rail tracks
That disappear into the horizon, into his pupils
He speaks of the midnight Special to Ft. Worth . . .

The Switchman for Rock Island disagrees
Says Burlington Northern is best
He smiles that we are carrying guitars and shows us the right
    track
It leaves at midnight for Texarkana

Laredo suggests leaving the freezing freight yard twilight
In search of warmth and Coffee
A Cobalt Northern has just come in with its tail in the Yukon
And its mighty head in our thin Lubbock jackets.

We walk a block behind the tracks
To see the house my grandfather built
Nostalgia pulls me into its vacuum
When I find nothing there but a vacant lot

Stranded like an island between a wrecking yard
And the chemical pool's plating garage.
Locked between the tracks of the Rock Island Line
And the blood flow of Mighty Route 66.

Around the corner was where the welders fired
Showers of comets from their torches
Warning children that to peek at the sparks
Was to be blinded forever.

The children always peeked.

Steel Machines waited in exile

And waited for the boys who hurled the rocks
Skeletons of earth moving creatures
Slept by the sulfur pools

And so I stand where I was conceived,
520 N.E. 3rd Street, Amarillo
In a vacant lot of goat-heads and milkweed
In a no man's land of derelict dreams

Here is where my father's seed found the gate
To my mother's garden
Once a place of lilacs and honeysuckle
Where the purple wisteria climbed the sun-bleached trellis

Here where the cedar fence stood
Lilac bushes exploded and roses flared.
Trimmed gardens edged with pride
Bloomed a haven safe from the anarchy of the universe

All of this was paradise.

For Sunday dinner my father would wring a chicken's neck
I would chase it around the yard
Crashing into fences in nerve-twitching panic
Slamming through the garden in search of its head
All hearts were innocent and all cups were full.

When a child, the world is Immortal
And all things seem Forever, Permanent
Here sat the ashtray, here was the divan
Here was the kitchen where we cooked the chicken

The piano hovered here, in the middle of the room
So mysterious it was, I thought I'd explode
The sparkling keys would dance
When Jimmy Meeks came to dinner

Hoboes would come to our back door
My mother could never turn them away

Their hungry eyes, their kind requests
Assuring us that better times were just ahead

The albino family lived across the street
I marveled at their pink eyes, pale skin and shyness
We played in the wrecking yard on rusty road graders
The smell of their steering wheels made our fingers turn black

This, too, was paradise

My Chinese friends, Kings and Wings
Would balance like tightrope walkers
On the fossils of this iron graveyard
The albinos were clumsy and stayed close to the ground

Kings was brave and showed me
How to dare great danger
By walking the catwalk under the underpass
Above the cars that whooshed in darkness

Wings drew pictures of the Mighty Superman
And showed me how to jump the gap
Between the garage roof and house
While little Barbara would applaud lustily

We built forts out of tumbleweeds
And spent long afternoons collecting nuts and bolts
The TV played Crusader Rabbit
And Gorgeous George, the Great Psychiatrist Wrestler

How the dishes rattled when the trains came in.
How the tracks echoed the thunder.
The whistle moaning a lonesome shriek
Heard citywide, from Grain Silo to Graveyard

The birds would scatter from the Elm and Ash
Dogs would bark, warning their Masters
Horses raised their ears, sensing faraway danger
Even the dying thought they had heard their last call

The Rock Island trains shook the earth from its sun
As the evening turned wheat fields crimson
New oil derricks lit up the somber landscape
Like launch pads in the alien, dusty West.

I have carried these visions with me
And applied them when surrounded or unsure
I have thrown pieces away not looking back
And waited in ecstasy till the dinner bell rang.

* * *

The sun sinks low. I'm a Vagabond on this street of memories
The cold reality emerges of Steel against Steel
The thunder of coupling cars, copulating,
The hiss of air brakes from the bowels of stark Weight Power

The massive sound transforms me
Into a lost romantic fool from an old Irish novel
Discovering the density of danger
With the innocence of frightened ears, Totally Awake

Laredo and me walk to a cafe on Fillmore
To escape the new cold blast of North Wind
The cafe is warm and alive, a refuge of a honky-tonk
With piney paneling and neon shelter

The owner, "Mom," is aiming her cue stick with one eye.
A cowboy in a dirty black hat is laughing, leaning on the table
Her son, Jimbo, notices us sketching in a notebook
And asks us if we'd sketch him

My drawing makes him look Chinese
And Laredo's drawing looks stained glass
All things look different
Through someone else's eyes

We hear mention of a joint, where we might pass the hat
And dig up some scratch for this megalith of a trip

We leave for the bar, half a block down.
I play guitar to refugees locked in a tiny galaxy.

I pass the hat for $10 in nickels, dimes and quarters.
We dance back down the street, walking lighter than before
New England is two thousand miles away
And we have $5 each. Not a bad head start.

We walk back thru the rail yards under a Buttermilk Moon
There is only one boxcar empty in this 99-car Hotel.
We find a hobo wrapped in a stack of cardboard
We shake him, carefully, to see if he's alive

He pops awake and cusses, who are you kids?
He jumps off the train, asking again what town this is
"Amarillo? Hell . . ." And walks into darkness mumbling back
    at us
"Silly bastards. Crazy, silly, bastards . . ."

There is a rumbling, intense expectation

This cold Iron Rhino is preparing to charge
Every noise staccato, symphonic, amphetamic,
Stadium huge drumbeats, like Big Iron hittin' Big Iron

Like a platoon of bass violins in the hull of an ocean liner
Every feeling electric, as the whistle pierces the night
This night of nights, we are stowaways in an American epic
As we hold our breath till the final whistle explodes

The Rhino eases off, gentle at first
Soon roaring like a cyclone, like cannons over water
Then rushing like a falling piano across wheat-land America
Proud, bold, stubborn, primitive, and powerful

Silo towns bullet by our open door
Heartland towns where people are simple
Where the God is Feared and Guns secure Freedom
And the train whistle is as trustworthy as a grandfather clock

The Amarillo brakeman had misled us a little
He said our car would be dropped in Childress
But Childress goes by like the blur of a flashcube
A few streetlights and a Doppler bell railroad gate

We build a fire in a barrel out of oily wood and cardboard
And the fire mutates into a smoke bomb
We lean our heads out the door to breathe
The upwind side of our face sticking to the wind

Laredo is falling asleep sitting up, his head nodding
With the bumps in the tracks and his face in a candle.
I keep watch on the highball, the mighty Iron Rhino
My brain beats against my skull in time with the rickety rails

What a great sidekick, I think to myself
Brilliant, homemade fountain of east-west paradox
Laredo the sage, unafraid, crazy as a loon
Flint-eyed spark of highway fire, born to ride.

Wichita Falls calls us to shore
We jump to firm ground and walk downtown
The Piccadilly Cafeteria chandeliers are comedic
A study in Plas-Tex India and linoleum Christian Vogue

We howl at these grand absurdities
And varnish our aching bones with Coffee-gratis. Gracias,
    Laredo
We stroll like ghosts in the chilly dawn
To the playground at the First Baptist Church

And throw down our sleeping bags, dew-side first
Assured that sleep will be long and deep
Too soon we wake to the sound of foreign chatter
German children playing soccer and laughing at the
    "Schlafensackers"

We wake in the afternoon and hitch a ride
With stoned G.I.s to the highway, headed east
Another ride in a burned-out oil digger's truck
The driver said he was "sort of a geologist"

He let us off in Henrietta
As the night began to fall
We camp in a field of Yellow Iron Caterpillars
Swapping lies until sleep wrestles us under

I dreamed that I was being born.
I could feel the dampness and I could see translucence
Like a flashlight shining through the blood in your hand
Through the womb in watery red light

When I woke before the dawn on Wednesday morn,
The moon was blurring through the plastic tube tent
Like my dream of a vision of birth
The air was clean as wet stalks of weeds

Dew was on the Caterpillar wheels
A consonance of clarity sends my mind to reeling

We see the sun rise from a skid shovel cab.
Magenta like the belly of a bruised mango

While breaking camp we notice
What we thought were limbs on a scraggly tree
Was really a chain of walking sticks.
Masquerading in defiance of predators

We get a morning ride to the highway
With a "good old boy" and his friend "Liberace."
Through boot city Nocona, Bonita and St. Jo
Hardly any words between us made time disappear

They let us go out on East Highway 82.
We throw rocks at fence posts and wait for hours.
Laredo says, "If we hit that hinge we got us a ride."
Within seconds, two rocks hit the hinge

Within minutes a ride appears
With two girls from Sherman, to bathe at their house,
Drink their music and Maxwell House Coffee
They then lay us down easy, back on the side of the road.

A three-hour wait buys us another ride
With a nervous brother and sister
That led to another in an ominous Black Diesel
Bringing us inside of the fair town of Bonham

Two black boys walk with us down the street eating bananas
"Where y'all comin' from and where y'all goin?"
I notice bushes on this street with strange shaped leaves
And clusters of red berries.

"Do you know what kind of bush this is," I ask
"That's a Red-Berry-Bush," he replied
The Skies lit up with Truth
And I vowed to follow It all the days of my Life.

We get a lucky ride with a black man and his wife.
They talk of Strength And Solidarity
Sanctuary in the Soul And Spirit,
Not even a mention of Toil And Trouble

They let us out at Sunset in Paris, Texas
In a clump of trees behind another truck stop.
There's a Rumor of rain. Fire and wine warm the purple night
We hope our plastic tent will keep our souls dry

Once again I'm thankful for a friend like Laredo
Here on the Back-Lot of life's stage
Nothing else matters at least till tomorrow
And the cogwheels of the
    universe click us to
    sleep one more time

The next day it rains like a
    snare-roll all day
We sit in the truck stop
    over Coffee & ball-
    points
Our ears are pulled back
    like those of wild deer
Who must sense each
    intrusion to survive in
    the wild

We walk toward Paris in
    an Oklahoma sunset
A car pulls up, "Hop on
    in!" says Wanda Jumper
She shows us her loop, her
    every night run.
We meet her wild-eyed
    friends at the Gibraltar
    Hotel

Where the Deskman had been since 1924
He said it hadn't changed since before '14
The Greek pillars are hysterical and give the illusion
Of a Slapstick Symmetrical, but Hobbled Eternity

We saw Paris from the eyes of a native.
I think Wanda was glad to have some new faces in town
Wanda left us money for a Texarkana bus
We left her a sketch of the Gibraltar Hotel

Towns roll by warped and starched with sun.
I dig for their history in any kind of visual clue
Who laid this brick street? Where are they now?
Who abandoned this church? Why is the School painted
    brown?

Texarkana is sad with welfare faces, stoic as rock
Arteries clogged with tankers for Houston
"Go Big Blue" scrawled in tempera on the telephone booth.
The Indian woman looks forever out the bus window.

The cold and rain is eating at our spirits,
The New England Fall seems too far, too cold
We flip a coin either North or South
Louisiana wins, we'll leave in the morning

There are no answers for gypsies who Question
Just questions, mysteries, mazes and riddles
And no good reason for any destination,
Other than living in the present

We get a ride the next day with Twin Racist Sisters
In a flatbed truck with tarnished baby moons
We just barely make it to Fouke, Arkansas,
Home of the famous Monster Burger

Fouke is not part of this world,
Rather it's a Piss-Stop on the road to Dante's vision of Hell

Wild pickups racing quarter horses in the streets
They talk of a Bigfoot who lives out back.

The public gathers in clumps
And it appears that Justice resides with the Biggest Clump
When Law and Politics sleep in the same bed together
Truth and Justice are the first to suffer

We flag down a white El Camino
A drunk man yells to get in the back.
He stops every five minutes to take a leak.
I remark that he must have one hell of a Bladder

"You got a problem with my bladder," he asks,
And takes a swing backwards with his one free hand.
Never have I seen anyone defend their bladder
With such fury and a clenched fist.

At the far end of his left hook he looses his balance
And tumbles backwards in the bar ditch
Pissing on himself like a Gulf Coast Gambler
Who's bet The Ranch and drew a Blank

Our instincts tell us to Split, but we're laughing too hard
The other man and his wife pull him in the pickup
And take us on to Shreveport, thank you Lord,
And drop us downtown at Dark.

We make it to the nightclub side, Bossier City,
In the prime of the winged-out night.
I play alternating sets with a stripper and pass the hat
I make 13 dollars in small change. Hot Damn!

I find Laredo with the poet's blues at the baseball park
And tell him about my change in luck.
We sleep under the bleachers in soggy sleeping bags
Till the sweet sun rises over 3rd base.

We ride back to Shreveport with an ex-hobo full of advice
He said that in his railroadin' days he had nothin'
"Now," he said, "I've got a beat-up pickup, 2 acres,
A wife and kids and 67 dollars in the bank."

We check out downtown, the Subway Cafe
We feast on our newly earned fortune
Devouring hot roast beef sandwiches
Upon the sunny balcony overlooking the World Jesus
    Convention.

We decide to head back to Bossier City
But the highway is a half-mile away.
In front of us is a railroad bridge over the Red River
Barely wide enough for one train.

We wait while the Eastbound goes across at dusk
Surely another won't be coming anytime soon.
We get halfway across and see the light of a train
Barreling down the tracks, turning into the bridge

Laredo climbs out on the side of the bridge,
A hundred feet above the water
Holding his suitcase and guitar
While I decide to high-tail it back to shore

I'm running on every other railroad tie
And my eyes get crossed up and I fall thru the space
Skinning my shin to my knee.
I was Saved from the Red River by my very own crotch

My guitar goes spinnin' down the tracks
Laredo had seen me runnin' so he started runnin'
He grabs my guitar and bee-lines it to the other side
The train is screechin' to a halt, sparks flyin' from the bridge

I limp across to the riverbank
Calling Laredo seven kinds of sons-a-bitches

He's in a ball laughing, kicking his heels in the air.
I have to laugh, it's too painful not to

We share some wine and weigh our odds
We spin a bottle and the bottle says, "Go!"
The Moon shines on the Silver Tracks and I have visions
Of an Iron Ladder to the Heavens

In the middle of the bridge is a Lookout Tower
With a platform panorama of all of Shreveport
The lights of the city and the red glowing clouds
Makes two fool Travelers seem that much more small

We roll out our sleeping bags in a run-down shack
And cross from one vast land into another
I dream I'm fishing with Joe Don and Wally
We snag a talking blue marlin who informs us that he's
    Siddhartha.

The 11:30 to Vicksburg shakes the shack
The boat rocks with an earthquake roar in my dream
We wake to reality of rust-hulled Boxcars
With enough open doors to exodus all Bossier City!

Our car beckons and we spring on like school kids
The coupling creaks as the train stretches a mile of steel
Every joint is tortured, even the wheels resist the roll
The Big Iron Rhino begins to charge as our senses reel

Soon we're sailing through the Cyprus in Old Louisiana
The sun is beaming down on Pine And Cotton
Farmers hoeing their crops, wild birds gathering seed
I feel completely in place, like a Spirit with new Batteries

I have found my sun, tho the orbit may be wild
Riding the wild rails with my face in the wind
Born of Freedom, I am returning again
To be set free by the very wind that imprisoned me

IRON RHINOS   57

We smell the Mississippi River miles before we arrive
The golden sky floods the atmosphere with Muddy River light
The rhythm of the wheels against the steel bridge
Beat with the heartbeat of the Planet

The crimson waters like a Juggler Vein
On course to the Heart of Gulf Salvation,
No closer to freedom have I ever been than this soft night
Watching the Sunset on the Mississippi River from an open
    Boxcar Door

We floated into the Vicksburg Ravine
And coasted in the train yards, no city in sight
The switchman wanted to know about our guitars
He radioed in to Central sayin' the Music had arrived

The Workers came from every corner of the Rail Yard
We sat on a cold flatcar playing train songs,
Songs from Woody, Hank, Muddy, and Elvis
Songs that had grown from this very Mississippi Mud

We passed a bottle of wine and swapped stories
Played songs from Texas and songs from Tennessee
And when the work whistle blew we all said farewell
And they asked where we were goin' and if we needed a lift

They called the Switch engine to bump us down a mile.
And said to hang on tight on this flatcar here
We held on for dear life, as the engine came down hard
Blasting us with a boom heard all over Vicksburg

We flipped, rolled and tumbled down the flatcar
At first we Cussed and then we Cheered
We coasted a mile down the levy, right to the steps to the
    heart of
    the city
They had given us the poor man's version of the Railroad Red
    Carpet.

We find Coffee at the hilltop Bar-B-Q
And play to the old black men who gather around.
They feed us our first meal of the day besides Laredo's crackers
We thought we were in Heaven surrounded by Black Angels

We went looking for sleep. The YMCA was too full
We were too late for the Salvation Army.
We lay down a pallet behind the church by Big Buck's cafe
And sleep like bears in Honey Town

Grits and Coffee give us that deep south feeling
We shower at the Army and find a Laundromat
Our poor clothes have gone on strike
After all, it's only been a week

Laredo makes 11 dollars at Tommy's Paradise Lounge
But at closing time all hell breaks loose
The Queen of the Mississippi takes a swing at Tommy
    Paradise.
And tells him he can stick "for Better or for Worse" sideways
    up
    his ass

I make it back to the churchyard and sleep in the vines.
Laredo takes his chances on the front lines
It's a restless night, no sleep for the sailors
The ocean is calling, the weather won't last

So long Vicksburg, you ain't much of a host
We've got a hot date with Destiny
And You've given us Less than Most.
There's a Silver City somewhere out there callin' my name

* * *

Cabeza de Vaca had bats in his head
That is why the natives liked him so
They taught him how to use lizards to track Destiny
In exchange for little Spanish Crosses made of tin

He carried on his exploration
In a suit of River Gourds And Sea Shells
When the Spaniards found him he'd become a Wise Man Of
    Medicine
Laughing Naked, dragging a bag of deer turds

We sail thru Jackson, in a blink of an eye
Then on to Canton, old time Slave City
Where the Ivy League was built on the Sweat of Africa
And the pale Southern Belles' breath smells of Pork and Mint
    Julep

Later in the day we snag a ride in a Xerox truck
With a man who has mapped every single pothole
From Memphis to New Orleans and back
His Winnebago is filled with shattered machines

He fires up the power and the Generator lights up
Laredo and myself have ourselves a little Xerox party
We Xeroxed our hands, faces and Levi Jackets,
As well as our thoughts, our dreams and empty-ass stomachs

When we step down in Memphis, the night feels like it's been
    packed away
We're already missing our asylum that we left behind
We walk ghostly Beale Street, cut over to the Highland House
    Rehab Center
Where they let us in to toss and turn in our own weary, beat-
    up kind of sleep

We shoot outa Memphis like a cat from a dog
To the town of the shoe box school
Where a solemn young teacher, wise in nylon stockings
Leads us with grace through the Tennessee fall

We coast down a smooth-as-leather Freeway
In balance with the Souls in the world
As quiet harmony settles over the trees, red and gold,
And we're thankful to the spirits who filled our Cup

Jackson again, Tennessee this time around
We drink franchise Coffee at the Scottish Motel
And eat fried chicken off the bone
Stolen from the throw-away World

Lawrence Brojic was a freeway pirate
Who howled pure disgust from the opening of the door
Who drove a rented car and pulled a U-HAUL trailer
And who threw me the keys within minutes of meeting

Lawrence of the North en route from Mexico
Ranting for hours, calling everyone a fool,
Every American a prisoner, every action fruitless
And, as if to add credibility, even added himself

Outspoken unromantic truth, he spewed
Hard as guardrails, as pounded asphalt
With eyes that were beaten like a yellow yard dog
Thrown into the ocean to learn the art of swimming

He sang of his beautiful Mexican women, each one his wife
Dreaming of retirement in humble Mexico
While aiming his total sperm at his capitalistic dream
Bursting like fireworks on the bombed-out highway

Lawrence, the hostage in his own prison
A product of the work-ethic factories he hates so much
A fill-in-the-pieces philosopher at war with jigsaw puzzles,
A knight in armor battling the Maya in the Mirror

He dropped us in Toledo with Good Luck and Praise
He opened his soul and gave to us his strength
Little did we know he was preparing us for Battle
In a city as hard as its Steel

Holy Toledo! We ain't got a dime!
It's four A.M. and we're hungry, cold and tired

IRON RHINOS

61

Watchin the big badass waitress spit orders from the refugees
To the Queasy cook in the Greater Toledo Greyhound Station

We walked in the rain and meet rainy people
One hard hit couple invites us to their shack
For sleep and eggs and newspaper story
Of a fallen baby, a raid, and years of bad luck

The freezing wind blows in
Through the cracks in the plaster walls
I hear a baby, far away, crying for its mother
I think of my own mother, far away, and cry my self inside out
    back to the womb

We get up in the late afternoon and walk downtown
Double-time broke, bumming Coffee And Cigarettes
Laredo passes the time mimicking the zombies on the bus
Scratching his armpits, expressionless

I leave Laredo in the Waldorf Lobby
And go to the Hillbilly bars and play songs
I play all night, six hours, and make $7 in loose change,
A sore throat and blisters on my fingertips

The characters I meet are unbelievable! Frenchy, Arce, Josey
They're the Rust Belt Depression Outcasts
Whose poverty has carved random canyons in their faces
And filled Deep rivers of sadness with their drunken hearts

Their friend, the Tennessee Rambler, invites us to his tragic
    home
There are French fries on the sheets and children on the floor
Singing songs about the sun and the cotton in Texarkana
While his washed-out princess just stares at the wall, defeated
    and weary

We knew we could never close our eyes in this sad-assed
    world
So we bid the Rambler family goodnight

And go next door for donuts and Coffee
Sorry that the Tennessee Rambler got lost in his own Spiritual
    shadows

We go for sleep to the industrial area of Toledo
In the icy backyard of the Great Lakes Storage Warehouse
Where the stars seem so far away, and the dirty ships so cold,
Where the rusty shipyard moans in the lost north wind

We froze to the bone as the wind cut deep
I packed my sleeping bag with every rag I had
When I did go to sleep, I dreamed
That the Tennessee Rambler had opened up his very own
    donut shop

We left Toledo to those more brave than ourselves
And smooth-sailed it into a Pennsylvania blowout
We then rode four in a Semi to Beaver Falls
And guzzled gallons of free coffee at the flat tire truck stop

I sang Banks of the Ohio and Monongahela Sal
While Laredo searched for his lost notebook
A saintly couple of W. Virginia folk Philosophers
Invited us in for tea and crumpets and our first warm night
    sleep since Vicksburg

We woke to cabbage fields and apple trees
On a sparkling Pennsylvania morn
Riding through the woods with Yvonne Marlier
And her soul mate, Amazon Ann

From the graveyard by the toll road
To Iron City, Pittsburgh, the Mighty Pit,
Where we waited hours for the next ride
From an ex-hitchhiking cop who couldn't spare a dime

Star-crossed and luckless in the Iron City Suburbs
Saved by the fruit monger, she gave us apples and Bread

She simply used her common sense
She saw our eyes were taking on the gaunt gaze of the Wolf

Laredo became a Marriage Counselor at the bowling alley
Selling 10¢ poems and advice, surrounded by bowlers' wives
I went looking for a Place To Play, anywhere
I got run out of the American Legion by a drunk

He says "here you goddamn bum, now get gone!"
He pulled out a Dollar bill and threw it on the pavement
He ground it into the asphalt with the heel of his shiny Brogan
    shoe
As if to say he liken my Being unto Gravel

I picked it up and straightened it out
And thanked him again and reminded him to breathe
Because his anger was making him into a fool
And strangling him in the cell he made for himself

I headed straight for the diner
And ordered soup and said a prayer for the old fool
And thanked the Creator for saving me again
The waitress smiled and brought stacks of crackers

She was like a river, Angelic & Liquid
The Legionnaire came in while I was slurping my soup
Two opposite people who Grazed My Life
Crossed in Time, Destinies Divided, Planets apart

I left the waitress a poem under my bowl
Beside the grains of salt and pepper
That told how opposite forces are necessary
So to cherish boundless love eternal

Laredo came in, excited about his discovery
That all bowling alleys could use a soothsayer
That is where mounds of problems lay hidden
Behind the roar of balls and clatter of pins

We were transported to a barn outside town
Where we rode a Stallion named Hombre
Around ancient stables, and felt the History of the Penns
And slept that night secure in that all was well again,
    somehow

It's back to the road with food in our bodies
With a ride that spoke not a word clear across Pennsylvania
Leaving us at the DC Exit with darkness falling
And a kind of peaceful uncertainty setting in

Laredo bummed cigarettes at the Highway Patrol Office
And, undaunted, went back for coffee
He claimed the coffee would produce an instant ride, which it
    did
All the way to the Garden State

The Rhode Island bartender filled our cups
And gave us tobacco and matches
We felt like we were safe and had rejoined the World
Watching Johnny Carson in a New Jersey tavern

We went to camp in the woods between two freeways
We tossed and turned, built a small fire out of cardboard and
    birch sticks
And tried to wrestle a restless sleep out of twisted dreams
And wrathful sounds from the Interstate

I woke to Laredo shouting in ecstasy
He had found an antique bottle of Tru Ade Soda
We kicked around the leaves and more were sleeping
In fact everywhere we looked were antique beverage bottles

We saw visions in our head of selling them on the streets
The Visions soon turned to Delusions of Wild Riches
As we found more, an old Creme Soda bottle, NeHi, Ginger
    Ale
A Dr. Pepper with the 10, 2 and 4 engraved in high relief,

We filled Laredo's Green Sack full to the brim
Laughing like hyenas at every discovery
This intersection must have slept for decade after decade
Protected by a wall of speeding iron

We must appear to be delirious madmen
Hitchhiking on the New Jersey Turnpike with a tow sack full
    of glass
A stoic Brooklyn army Sergeant gave us a ride to Elizabeth
Where we took turns lugging the bottles street to street

"We don't even buy new bottles, much less muddy ones"
Said the grocer seconds before he ran us out
"Get outta here before I call the cops," said the antique dealer
There's gotta be some mistake we said, these bottles . . .

The liquor store, the pawn shop, the street pimp
No one knew the value of our excavations
If we had a quarter, we could have called an Archaeologist
But, sigh, we were still dead-ass broke

We dropped the sack with a crash on Elizabeth's streets
And staggered back to the highway, head down
I do not remember the face who took us over the river
Thru the Gates of the Silver City, Harlem burnished like
    broken glass

Survival forced our attention
Away from aesthetics, away from beauty
Little did we notice that the leaves we came to see
Had stealthily fallen from the trees

And in doing so had declared that winter
Was breathing down our Texas necks
And that the safety we had left behind in dear ol' Lubbock
Was now just a memory, a hundred Best Westerns away

Nor do I remember much about the first few days in the city
We slept on the Staten Island Ferry, played songs on the streets

Hallucinated phone numbers on the sidewalks
Froze our fingers blue, and prayed for mercy

I could hear the Big Iron Rhinos all around me
Under the earth, in the skies, rumbling in Skyscrapers
The rumbling of men's machines that had awakened in me as
   a child
Had carried me to a city built by Giants

I looked up past the Chrysler building
Up through the canyon walls
I saw the same Orion that had guided my travels
And it made my body tremble and it filled my soul with Iron

LUBBOCK TO MANHATTAN
Fall 1972

BONFIRE OF ROADMAPS

(Xpedition Impossible)

Imagine a room full of eggbeaters and hornets
Imagine that they are all churning
Driven by a noisy engine with bad bearings
And amplified by a cheap P.A.

Survival has forced me to tolerate confusion
My house has become a switchboard,
An information booth full of glossy pamphlets
Embossed with maps to the inner hurricane

I've surrounded myself with machines that talk
They answer my phone, they remember my voice
Like narcissus, they feed my ego with pleasure
Until some circuit shorts and stirs the electronic water

Lately the water has been boiling
And the phone never stops ringing
If it weren't for love and music
I might simply "unplug"

To add to this crowded situation
I decided to tour EurØpe like a Gypsy
With my band of compadres
And a stack of raging songs still wet.

It must have been a madness
That overcame me in my sleep
I own a long history of fighting flame with fuel
To escape the cell by reminding the jailer of his workplace

Here we go . . .

So many times I've crossed this ocean
In the belly of a metal bird
So many times I've watched the moon
Rip across the sky as if it were sliding on ice,

Lighting the tops of ocean clouds,
Sailing ships and tankers
Flying fish, sharks and marlins,
Pirates and smugglers and the crazy albatross

And so we land in a London fog
Tangled up in sleeplessness and apprehensions
Prepared to tackle 28 rowdy days
Of back stages and border crossings

We fought off jet lag with Indian food
And met our crew under a black bridge
We tested rental amps and the whole building shook
When blue trains rattled the ancient brick

They told us—"Shut it off, Goddamnit"

I slept like a bag of sand
And woke to shocking English memories
Of wild crowds covered with steam
And brilliant white light spilling out into the rain

I walked through Kensington Gardens
Feeling I could use a revelation
And when none came I took a leak at the gazebo
As Botticelli's Venus came jogging by.

Back at the hotel, the band was getting ready
The phone rang, "The bus is here."
The silence was drop-dead when the reality of travel sank in
All the gear and 8 of us in a Fuckin Fiat truck

The Dingwalls gig was loud and harsh
The walls were stone, the ceiling was stone
And pretty girls on the front row
Turned red and green I heard the bells of Camden Town
    ring . . .

We played the Mean Fiddler under amber light
And old Clash friends and Portobello rebels stopped by
Their girls got light headed and danced on the checkered
    tables
While the men guzzled grain bier in green bottles

At 4 A.M. we crawled in our red bus
And began our expedition to eurØpa via the port of Dover
Screeching tires and crashing metal outside London
Was only the first premonition that we were in for a fight

The white cliffs loomed dreamlike
And dizzy in our dirty windows
Like vertical clouds climbed in sleep
They rose from the fog like Freon from a forgotten lake

We drove into a huge white ship
Directed by men with orange sleeves, slinging rope
The diesel whale slipped from the dock
I watched Dover recede into a mist I'd probably never see
    again . . .

There was meat being fried all over that ship
Even a sea gull could track our breath
Wake up boys, for the 4 o'clock pork on the North Sea
Let's sing "90 miles of bad water" in 8 part harmony

We land at Zeegrube in quaint little Belgium
And make our way to Holland
Banging our heads against the window
Sleeping sitting-up, well below sea level

The cloudy Paradiso still stands
I remember my first trip to EurØpe
Dancing naked in a wonderland
Populated by hash bars and black bicycles

The Paradiso had many rooms then
Each filled with red cluster fantasy
I painted the tops of buildings
And learned to swallow live herring at Scheveningen

I remember the man who gave me a book
After the performance one red night
He spoke in a whisper, said he was moved
Weeks later I had the feeling that his whisper was no more

Now again we play the rock church
The audience of Dutch stare and sway
Grissom plays like a man possessed
The improv gene screamed from his fingertips

And when Davis and Jimmy the Bump
Locked in on the Bottom End
The gears of the Universe merged
With a rhythm that revealed every secret ever concealed

Twice our van was broken into
By blind junkie desperadoes
They took the tape player from the dash
They left David's blue boots and Mike's white computer

By the time we hit the road we were laughing like sailors
Singing "no rules on my trip"
But the laughter turned to groans
After a freezing two hours at the German border

Strange Rows Of Lights Crawl Past The Windows
Industrial Germany with its angular fluorescence
The aspirin factory goes on for miles
The throbbing bus bleeds diesel from boredom

Our humor turns cynical as we inch across the map
Two hours crawl by in mystery
Stranded on the autobahn penned like cattle
In this red Fiat psycho jail

Time becomes brutal, I laugh at shadows
What the hell am I doing?
I never set out to be a nomad martyr
In some EurØpean rock and roll hell.

Patience wears thin after the sun comes up
No sleep and a 3-hour delay at the Swiss border
My mind drifts and bends
Memories of the theater marching from Paris to Vienna.

EurØpean history is full of bastards waiting
Entangled in bureaucracy
Here we are at this end of the wire
Under mountains of paper and data

I have the same feeling as when I was in jail
On the top floor of the old Lubbock county
Only instead of iron bars, there are borders of countries
Instead of jailers there are government dickheads

I fall into a Swiss goose bed at noon
And dream bizarre scenes of asphalt and guardrails
I see Mickey Mouse on my computer lit in neon
Joking about the un-history of eternity

I can't remember ever being deeper in sleep
I was a forgotten car at a wrecking yard covered in snow
Hearing a faraway ring I thought it was angels being rude
I woke with gravel in my eyes to a chirping telephone

"Get up! you must be on TV in an hour"
"Look your best! The cameras want your image"
So down we went to Swiss chrome modern Studio
Run by pushy little men with beady eyes

I somehow locked myself in the dressing room
So I climbed out the 2nd floor window
I lost a button on my coat and scuffed my boots
I was ready to fight when I entered the TV Studio

The host did an interview with the man and the woman
Who had flown non-stop around the world
They talked about fatigue and I listened intently
Like a sculptor carefully inspecting his welding torch

We did not watch the replays, we headed for food
Like wolves in a pack showing wet teeth
We tested our mics and went to the basement
Where we dressed in a room brown with musty lockers

I suppose the gig went well
I only remember the heat and the light
And the blond kamikaze drunk at the front
Who uttered not a peep when I stepped on his hand

When we packed up and left, I didn't want to go
I wanted to wake to the bells of Zurich
Maybe I had a premonition of what was to come
The bus pitched and rocked in the pitch black Alps

South to the border where the Italian Police waited

It was 7 A.M. when we crossed the border,
The coffee was thick and black and hot
The truck drivers gathered and joked and smoked
While we waited for our number to light up on the sign

Back and forth from the bus to the bar
We looked at our clocks and then at the sun
And while it scraped the Alps on the Italian side
It hurt our eyes in no man's land

The last sleep we'd had was in Amsterdam town
Two days away, though it seemed like a week
Our number came up at the crack of noon
I slumped in my seat and braced for the ride.

Father Phil, the driver, came shaking his head
"Son-of-a-bitches," he said, slamming the door.
"The chief of police has just gone to lunch,"
"International traffic will just have to wait."

"Shit!" I said, and saw my breath,
The cold was starting to work its way in

Like a corkscrew straight to the core of our nerves
The truck yard reeked of frozen diesel—10 below 0

The police chief returned an hour late
Laughing with his flunkies and rubbing his belly
Like a pig who'd just eaten a bushel of corn
Picking his teeth with a dirty fingernail

He signed the papers and suggested we proceed
A hundred yards deeper down a crawling yellow line
Our carnet must be stamped by the customs official
To emancipate our guitars from this mozzarella quicksand

Phil returned again, hands up in the air
What now? What the hell else can it be?
"The asshole's gone to take a nap!"
"The bloody bastard's gone home to take a nap!"

John, his sidekick, the quiet one
Attacked everything Italian
The bus seems to sink—the bass amp plays taps
We were starting to feel like prisoners of war

Joe Sublett hit the nail on the head
With his Chaplin-like imitation of Hitler,
If it wasn't for him we might have strangled each other
Or else be impaled in Italian barbed wire

To live on the road you must have humor
It's like self-defense, like worldly karate
To admit you're a fool takes wisdom and courage
Not to mention vanity and lunatic stupidity

And So We Sit Like Patients In A Ward
Until Phil returns with a gleam in his eye
"We'll have to run the gate, we have no other choice"
"We'll bluff our way through, just hang on tight."

He fired up the Fiat and crept to the border,
We looked down our noses like diplomats,
But they picked us off like Gypsies wearing wigs
Swearing they were members of parliament

If this were a western, you'd say we were "snake bit"
If this were a drama we'd be "up shit creek"
If this were a comedy the audience would be roaring
When we u-turned to return to the end of the line

They ordered us out and took away our passports
And went through the bus like flies on a Big Mac
The guards were smug and cracked private jokes
Their Italian pistols where their peckers should be

Three hours later they let us go
We were still seven hours from our destination
Showtime was ten, we should be there by one
At least we'll have a good story to tell

We race through Italy, through Milan and Turin
Where the ancient shroud lay guarded by cops
If Jesus were alive, he'd be crying on the hillside
Things most precious need no armed protection

Through traffic jams, tollgates, detours and border checks
We stutter and stammer and shiver as one
Too cold to sleep, too tired to think
We enter the beauty of France at the stroke of midnight

A curved coast of lights, we see golden Monte Carlo
Bridges spanning valleys on the Cote d'Azure
Wishing for a moon, a meteor or comet
Any celestial light to let us be witness

We dress in the bus at sixty miles per hour
Slamming into walls, dancing on one leg
To arrive at the club met by happy talking faces
"Tre surreal" like fish in a jewelry store

We are on at two-thirty, four hours late
All that's left are drunks with cigars
Trying to put the make on the cocktail waitress
Lyle Lovett comes stormin' out the stage door as we walk in

The promoter had dropped a naked lady in a swing
Down on to the stage in the middle of a slow song
I was hoping the same thing would happen to us
The show like a dream separated by glass

We walk to the hotel down dark French streets
The shutters and the street lamps smell of French tobacco
Mixed with salt from the Mediterranean breeze
The echoes of footsteps bring memories of Villion

I have a wild sleep; I dream making love in a bathtub
With love pouring like watercolor splashing to music
A symphony of sea gulls tap dancing in tuxedos
With Spanish dancers clapping exploding castanets

I wake like lead in the late afternoon
And have coffee with Davis at the bar-tabac
A lady takes her poodle from her zippered purse
And pets it drinking coffee, then zips it up and leaves

It's hard to believe we have a day with no travel
I'm not sure I'm ready for such grand luxury
Part of me is hanging from the ceiling by my ankles
Praying that a miracle will fall out of my pockets

France is like a string of pearls
With a peacock painted on each
Tho stained with tobacco they look good at night
When chandeliers shine on cracked plaster halls

And the girls all sing, la la ooh la la
It's intoxicating here on the southern coast
Where Van Gogh lost his ear to illusions of beauty
Where sycamore trees twist all in a line

If I stayed here any longer I would lose more than an ear
They'd find me at the beach eating my palette of paints
Chasing them with champagne, gazing toward the harbor
Where Polanski's phantasmal pirate ship waits

The night before I leave I dream a dark hallway
I'm between a palm tree and a fire escape window
Checking out the stopped clock at the train station
Frozen in romantic suspense by the walking trees of Arles

I wake at 6:30 for the 7 o'clock train
And ride the dark coast to the station at Nice
We walk in a pack in a blue freezing wind
The doors of an airport never looked so good

I think of Phil and John and dedicated Palsce
Bumping across Germany in that damned red Fiat
This flight will save the soul of the band
From the asylum for musicians at Newcastle

We change out planes at Paris, De Gaulle
And write a paragraph to loved ones on Eiffel tower postcards
We drink strong coffee from porcelain vessels
And hear electronic bells from the respiratory speaker

We wait in Copenhagen for hours and hours
Hoping the crew hasn't run into trouble
We try to sleep on airport seats
But a videotaped cartoon loops loud and insane

When the crew arrived, we sigh relief
We are starting to think in terms of disaster
We love what we're doing, we whisper over and over,
As to convince ourselves each night, in theory.

Muddy Waters once said to me,
22 hours of misery, 2 hours of ecstasy
I pinched myself, hoped to god it wasn't true
A big red bruise popped up on my arm

I think of sweet innocent Lubbock
And people asleep, safe within their jobs
Why did I choose this strange occupation?
To tell you the truth, I wouldn't do nothin' else.

On the ferry to Sweden the ocean is frozen
The ferry cuts a channel through salty slate ice
The gig is bland, we're really not with it
It's so far from France and sweet sunny Texas

My girls are just waking in their king size bed
They stretch and yawn and nuzzle in pillow
And perhaps think of me in the frozen north
And look with love into each other's eyes

Next morning we take the last train to Stockholm
And restlessly walk from car to car
The countryside is white and dotted with gray
The train packed with stern Aryans, unamused.

All I recall is the dinky-assed elevator
From the club to the basement
Wired for burglars and guarded by some skinny kid
The hard rock, Sweden, was made for burgers not guitars

I talked to old friends, Urban and Karin
Finally in their own austere city
Here, I could understand their temperament
They seem so out of place in tropical Austin

We drove the next day to Oslo and the Hotel West
The icy north has got the city surrounded
I wake up early the next morning and walk six hours
And study these Vikings, this distant culture

An American in EurØpe is a cultural amputee
The icons of TV land that we grew up with are invisible
Simply unable to replace what was built by hand
And passed on alongside living history

I walk by the palace all lost in thought,
Kicking snow with my high top gray tennis shoes
A group of people was gathered on the steps
Examining what looks like a multicolored kite

I introduce myself as a balladeer from Texas
Just taking in the sights till the concert tonight
One man with a cane introduces all the rest
He saves for last, "His majesty, the King of Norway!"

I can't believe it, the King of Norway!
Just walkin' down the street and I meet the King of Norway
I shake his hand and say, "I can't believe this!"
"It's very nice to meet ya, your honor"

He asks about the concert and about our tour of EurØpe
I reply half-lying, "We've had the time of our lives"
Then, quite by surprise he offers to show me around
In the streets of old Christiania

In the Royal Garage is parked his Buick
We drive through the gates past guards with fur hats
And slide around corners on the gray icy streets
While I study the medals that adorn his suit coat

He pulls out a flask of fine Finnish vodka
And takes him a slug and hands it to me
I refuse him politely, explaining myself
"I'm a cactus man when I've got fresh limes"

We neither talk politics or about rock
In fact the whole conversation involves the female body
He asks what I think of the girls of Norway, I reply,
"I'd hump a bar ditch if I thought it had a drain."

We laugh and we slide around treacherous February streets
Broad-sliding once into a Volkswagen beetle
No harm was done, it just took off some paint
Not to mention the bumper with German plates

He goes on and on about western movies
Not a subject that lifts me out of my seat
I ask him if he'd drop me by the concert hall sound-check
Down at the docks by the bow-tie shop

And so I parted ways with the king of Norway
Him going his way and me going mine
It's amazing the coincidences that this world offers
When you cast your fate to a red Fiat truck

I didn't tell a soul about my amazing encounter
Who'd believe me? They'd say, "Well, there goes ol' Joe."
So I told 'em "I ate swordfish that stunk like a camel
And threw up cranberries in the Oslo bay"

The gig that night was at a legendary nightspot
For the life of me I can't remember the name of it
We blew the dust out of the acoustic tiles
And my ears rang like cymbals till the rising of the sun

We ate where the Vikings used to spill their beers
Where the moose would come out of the wall on the hour
And make some ridiculous crack and more beer would spill
And, like everywhere, people were proud and drunk with
    tradition

The next day I drove with Øyvind to the park
That the mad artist had covered with twisted bodies
The tower that he built was an erection to the arts
As if the somber intellect had iced over the wall of the heart

We said farewell and headed out for the port of Trondheim
In a Mercedes van following the lip of the spoon
The mountains rose quickly and the roads shrunk in width
The arctic snow began to fall when we turn up the ridge

In conversation, Father Phil is an interesting fellow
But when it comes to driving he devolves into a beast
Where the Road we travel becomes a fresh killed squirrel
He attacks with the fury of a starving wolf

So the last hundred miles becomes a battle of nerves
As we slide around icy roads inches from fjord free-fall
The rock and roll fast lane, around dead-man's curve,
We barely miss a moose, just as we see the lights of
    Trondheim!

Delirious, I jump ship and walk around talking to myself
I am convinced I'll hop an African tanker out of here

I walk for hours until my limbs are numb
I conclude a warm bed might be better for tonight

I wake in a wooden room with needles in my skull
With no memory of how I got here
By sound check I'm a werewolf, pitiful and pale
I prowl around the curtains like a hunchback with a clubfoot

The student center is round and Babylonian
By the second song the psychosis had vanished
As a circuit closed in my head, the electric snake awoke
And crawled through the building, eyes on fire, lunatic-like

I walked with Davis the next frosty morning
Through quaint streets that wound up the mountainside
The smell of the warm bookstore filled me with memories
As the blowing snow swirled between the colored houses

Wc walked up the hill to the old stone fort
The gentle snow became a blinding blizzard, then cleared
Even the granite turned chalky as Bayer aspirin
The harsh angles of the grandfather fort became soft and wise

Oh, holy rugged Norway chilled in white
Clear, curious, sad, self-preserving
The lonesome eyes of old sailors
Watching the shine of red cheeked schoolgirls

Wooden houses lean on stone stilts painted reds and browns
Whose tile roofs are deep in blue snow
Holding safe the stories of winter, the secrets of lovers
Snug in the stone valley, safe in the fingers of Mother Sea

The snow settled gracefully, angelically calm
We walked to the church to warm our hands
And were handed a program by a priest in robes
We had stumbled on a wedding so we acted "late"

The voice of the priest echoed sharp from the stone

The reverb overlapped the spaces between vows
Like voyeurs, we watched the couple come down the isle
Lit by harsh lights from a lone video cam

That night we played the Rowdies bar
A Trondheim motorcycle club with Harleys by every table
But the bikers had drunk too much of their own moonshine
And spilled it on their girls as they spun deranged

Before long they were peeling off their clothes
Making love right there, in front of the band
Pink Norwegian asses bobbin in un-harmony
Like corks in a bottomless lake

Back in the van headed south to Molde
We encountered the land of the Kamikaze Fjord Walkers
Walking down the middle of the snow-covered highway
Following arrows on signs reading, "Phsykotik Jukehaus"

We played the ballroom in Molde beneath crystal chandeliers
Miles Davis's ghost peeked out of the kitchen
The Moldenese clapped five beats to the measure
And raised their beers high over their heads

I had had it with the road so I waited for the boat
And walked around the village with a little black camera
I took picture after picture of pastel reflection
Never realizing my camera was empty of film

We missed the first boat, me and father Phil
So I walked even more outside the town down a grove of trees
I realized it was my birthday in the middle of a trance
Eyes transfixed on the eventuality of death

We got on the boat with a thousand school kids
Laughing, mischievous and armed with beer
I found my bunk and went to sleep
Just as the wind decided to blow

I woke up in mid air in a jet-black room
Thinking I had died and gone to space
Not a nebula one could I distinguish
When gravity called me home, I responded with obedience

All night long, I dreamed of space
Swinging from the stars like an ape
The smell of coffee was proof the ship was still afloat.
As I breathed in the beautiful bay of Bergen

Like a Technicolor postcard, Bergen smells of bread
Her streets are full of fish and pencils
She is blonde and poses for you in the streetlamp, nude
Her white horses nibble on clover growing by her father's
    rusty black bicycle.

The club was a cave, a hideout in World War II
When Hitler's goons were touring the coast
It was here he played the bongos while London burned
And broke out in blisters at the smell of frying meat

I could've stayed here and slept a week
This west coast of Norway has a way with your heart
Blushing, fresh, inquisitively innocent and hedonistic
Everything a man in a straitjacket could want

But I left the next morning on a hydrofoil hotrod
And watched Bergen fade into the hand of the mountain
As if the fjord had slowly closed her hand
Around the hand of her wondering child

Stavanger looked like a set from a cyberpunk novel
Orange lights and pipes reach from the sea like a launch pad
Like a man-made heart the size of a bank
Drinking oil from the bay to feed the veins of EurØpe

My exhaustion circles me like a buzzard
My whole soul is in pain, like a smokestack it steams
Too much music is sure to make you feel dead
And boil your brain to lima beans

I've been smoking big black cigarettes
And dreaming magnetic cars that hover like dragonflies
When you live like a conquistador, you cease to feel
The daggers of the world that fill every pore

Everybody's dreams have become bizarre and prophetic
Coochie dreams skulls, Jimmy the Bump dreams dashboards
Phil dreams Nashville with old men in hats
Playing sessions with computers and samplers

John the Brave dreamed about killer whales
Disguised as cute furry kittens sitting on his shoulders
And as they were about to tell him the secret of the universe
Somebody knocked on his jail cell for a wake-up call . . .

So back to Oslo for a benefit for Tore Olson
Who died in a car before his time

Now, who will be the one who will set fire to rock?
And bring exotic music to the north?

We come into Göteborg again 3 hrs late
The Poseidon has been cancelled, we walk to Excelsior
Things are haywire we are slowly shorting out
A record company is calling inviting us to dinner

The sound check called off, they can't hold the doors
We enter the dungeon down meat-packer stairs
My god, I can't do it, I've been through this before
My throat is meat and my sting is miles behind me

Father Phil is losing it boys
He's talking in riddles, his eyes are rolling
We meet in the basement to hear his plan
The drum roll begins for the exodus finale

It would have been so easy had we not missed the boat
Now we have to drive the length of Denmark
Temporarily stealing a Mercedes truck
His eyes roll back, "It's going to be close."

My hands are shaking, I stare at the seat back
There's a vice on my temples, my spine is a corkscrew
Twisting my guts, my lungs, my ribs
Passing every thing in sight, inches from disaster

I look at my palms, at the creases like highways
I see bridges, runways, and dead-end streets
Oh, love oh love across the sea
Do you ever think of me?

"We'll never make it," father Phil keeps saying
"It's the last boat to Harwich, no crib for a bed."
I feel I've been poured into a plaster cast
Dreaming of geisha girls and Shanghai opium

The drums have long since lost their rhythm
They battle each other to the rules of war
Timpani and snare, bass drum and cymbals
In a great iron warehouse without window or hinge

Then suddenly we're there, at a huge white ship
With its mouth still open and its ramp still down
We crash through the pylons and into its throat
And all bail out for the exodus from EurØpe!

We pick the truck clean like vultures on amphetamines
Amps and guitars, we throw against the wall
Drums, cases, and boxes of bolts
We pile in a fury in the ships' parking garage

"We made it!" we dance, and watch with awe
As Phil backs up the stolen Mercedes
"Piece of cake," says John Steele, ever so cool
Phil makes it back as they're cranking up the hatch

We take the elevator, to hell with the stairs
To the deck of the massive ocean ferry
Walking on air, starry-eyed with relief
Feeling we've just passed through the pearly gates

I buy me a bar of fine Finnish chocolate
And chase it with hot boiling coffee
And observe with confusion the nice orderly people
Roaming like cattle, contented, unamused

I found my bunk and slept hard as asphalt
Rocking on the sea like a newborn child
Events of the past were like nightmares on billboards
I honked and waved as we floated past

I awoke at dawn to a majestic sunrise
I saw two riders in the clouds riding reindeer
Flanked by rabbits in silly silver helmets
Over the gold tipped, green-black water

And I stretched in my bunk, clutched in this moment
Watching this golden light pouring on the sea
Headed back to mother England, to rock in her arms
Feeling lucky as hell, with a newfound faith

At Harwich in England we were surrounded by cops
Our method of arrival seemed suspiciously unorthodox
They kept our passports and confiscated our gear
Till John and Phil assured them this was not an invasion

From here on I'm hazy, I'm not sure quite what happened
I've been told that we played that night in London
The next thing I remember I was back home in Austin
With my shirt on backwards talking to cedar trees

I saw in the paper the Zeegrube ferry had sunk
Hundreds had drowned in the icy north sea
I wasn't surprised, I had a feeling disaster was hungry
And sniffing our tracks with his snout

A week later there arrived a letter from Oslo
The Hotel West had burned to the ground
It was probably some poor bastard drying his socks
With a bonfire of road maps in the bathroom

TOUR OF EUROPE
January thru February 1987

ONE FUSE OF A SUMMER

I walked down a spring wash on an Easter-like day
Runners, lovers, cooks, bloom'd construction
Tried to outrun the Colorado
Slept till Explosives at Continental

Watercolor and TV mixed hotel room
Birthday bar party in bleak firehouse bar
Played pool with banditos
Rode chase on a bus to Manchaca and nightmare

I lost a day on bad repair
Therefore, bored, broke fluorescent sticks on elevator
And sloshed wild on walls
Ate Mex food and laughed at flat tires and rain

I dreamed clod fight with the Rockefellers
He on a San Francisco hilltop, had a strategic advantage
It was a happy little game until the girl I'm with
Gets hit on shoe with brick mortar

I watched Newman rip innocent hardwood
To build a fiery guitar
To create a massive disturbance
Or calm a shattered heart

Fire trucks echoed in Austin fog
As I shot pool nonstop
Overdubbing shakes the pool house wall
The night sweats lust with sultry blues

Visions of neon train howling thru Texas nite
A self-contained circus, hotel and billboard
I'm wild with full moon Jesus
We mix howling snake blues tonight

8-cent baseball carries us away
To the realm of right and left brain
Dual steel guitars rocks D-day
At the Beans bar patio

4 A.M. went to find Banks for wit
He said psychologists have a name
For those who gather in kitchens
Late at night, night after night

I painted an account of the night,
The drugstore on 50th with 4 booths,
The furniture store that burned,
Rockets over airplane hangars

The headlines said *ATOM BOMB HITS PARIS!*
In reality a volcano had scatter'd transatlantic ash
Shooting blue lightning between the craters
Owners said the volcano was *not for sale*

The next day was lost in void of studio
Hours seem like minutes and
Minutes are magnified into colossal memory
As the studio takes on its own personality

The engineer works like a fine surgeon
Delicately stirring the ingredients
Night falls; the studio cat prowls
As sound is mixed with sound

A bass becomes a truck swerving with sleep
The steel burns red liquid in an elevator shaft
The drums chug as if the night had notches,
A clutch that slips, and a new brake job

Sun's up, time to sleep, sun's down, better get up
To watch sorry TV with the hotel shades pulled
Down to the Alamo, Butch is full of spark
We mix Brain Lock, eat shrimp and scream till 8 A.M.

We mix Hopes and Boxcars
We mix Brain Lock and express it to L.A.
We mix and mix and mix it's just not fair
My patience is thin like cymbals

I'm weary from the speakers, hammered with sound
I don't wanna get up. Passive about the control(z)
Live recordings are spiked with maya illusion
Nothing can be done now, I must give up

Leaving austin spring blooming child-like joy
Experience batter'd sequence circular time!
Blap! Goes a tiger-stripe butterfly on vw windshield
My time given lately to conceiving conception

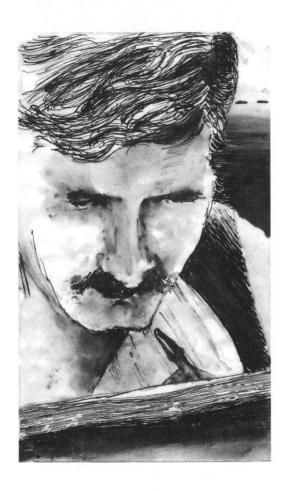

Girl in supermarket reading modern romance
I see pink bubblegum wrapper on side of road
It blends with colors of spring blossoms
I'm returning home, I'm returning to dust

Barbed fences curves caution: 40 mph
I can make it at 55. Body not right throat hurts, jaws
I haven't smoked since wrecked hot motel
This is a free country; one can drive as slow as they please

I pass the spot where I hang glider'd
And was overwhelmed at nature's contrasts

ONE FUSE OF A SUMMER

The textures of trees, bark, and Spanish moss
Scrub cedar and yucca over God's rocky cliffs

I've missed Texas spring for two years now
I've missed clearing of mesquite, cliffs of Llano
Paintbrush, bluebonnets, cactus fence, pecan bottom
Carcass of skunk and deer, pig farm and river

Vulture landing on limb of dead tree
I lit cigarette by antique store and rolled down window
At the courthouse of Llano silver roof
Cowboys and bull riders hint of things to come

My mind drifts back to past month in England
Maneuvering narrow roads, roundabouts
With drivers quick, solemn, classical and impatient
Troubled and proud, country that once ruled the world

I remember the windmills of Stonehenge
Barns, ponds, chimneys and fat sheep of a mild winter
I remember the color of the light
As it cut valleys in the faces of farmers

I read this morning about the need we have
Of a pure full band spectrum of white light
How your eyes drink it like healing nectar
Absent from fluorescent, incandescent and blue TV.

I read Baptist pamphlet over coffee in Brady
Comparing local miracles with ancient ones
One testimony was from a deer hunter
Whose engine block froze. Wham! It repaired itself!

Another had to do with standing still
(With reference to scripture)
While a tornado raced by double-dodging the family of faith
This is nothing new, this is my life

I drive on to Santa Anna of the mystic mesa
I add a qt. of oil singing breezes Indian breath
On to Winters, watch dogs chase chrome wheels going crazy
Seeing their image the same but wheel goes round and round

The Happy Piggly Wiggly sign smiles at a trucker
Checking the air in his tires as a cop gasses up
The State Theatre shut down by television
Sign says airport one mile—Cropdusters International

The smell of gasoline makes my nostrils flare
And my hair lay back. The sun glares in the west
I add shades, coloring the pure light
I have my own theories about creation

I awaken to Lubbock crumbling
Hatch said roadie quit, gone to El Paso
Mark sick, mother in the hospital, all looks bleak
The night coiled in tension, attacked by fame

I went to Gregg's then to Robert's, no relief
Sharon said leave my house, she was serious
I wandered delirious at 7-11 and vacant lot
The weeds are breathing, the stars whisper *fool, idiot*

Felt bad Saturday and the dust was blowing
The air electrical and shocking negative static
The dust settled at rusty dusk and the band played
The music hot and the night went on until daylight

Slept late Sunday and went to the hospital again
Mother was doing better so I took in a movie, Black Stallion
Visual romantic sentimental tears of relief
Went to Stubbs to jam and TV's late night

Shot pool 4 A.M., accidentally insulted a black hustler
He hit me in the jaw and then reconciled
I studied this dangerous creature as we moved
To more dangerous joints in darkest Lubbock

Saw Eddie Beethoven at Broadway Drug
He showed me totem poles and woodworking tools
His mind is galactic but born in the wrong century
He wants to build monuments out of 2 × 4s

I dreamed for 3 days I needed the rest.
I went to Spain and rented a rubber Citroen
Tires inscribed with *Each Man Becomes the Road He Takes*
I was trying to avoid secret lovers of presidents

Sharon's wild, she cries day and night
"You're irresponsible," she screams
"Yes," I say, "I've misplaced everything."
"And don't really give a damn if I find it."

I returned to the hospital my mother worse
Ice packs and antibiotics and endless lists
She asks me to cancel Amarillo, doctors are torturing her
I feel so helpless, I pray for a miracle

I have inherited her distrust for doctors
She is the perfect mother for the life of a seeker
Passionate, suffering, visionary and weak
Life stacks the deck in certain games of solitude

Morning with Smokey, I leave to the land of my birth
Quick stop in Plainview for used store shirts and tux
On to Amarillo in a vicious wind in a VW
45 mph top speed wall of north dust, sandpaper air

Scene: Amarillo honky tonk red and black
I drink a beer as the band tunes for 30 min.

First beer in 5 days, tastes good, no sound check
The club feels ominous, wish I were down the road

We open with *Hopes Up High* full tilt
This bull has its head down. Take no prisoners.
I notice a disturbance on Jesse's side of the stage
His amp was crackling; he'd just gotten shocked

He's ok, the show misses not a beat
Next song the stage sparks and quakes
Jesse's eyes wide, mouth foaming,
Falling into Lloyd's steel, hands frozen on electric guitar

Slow motion spastic muscles
Dissonant chords flying chrome
Lloyd knocks Jesse's guitar away from electric snake
The dance floor stops and stares

The song self-destructs, we turn to Jesse
"Shit! You ok", "Man, what was that?"
"Try it again?" "Hell, I guess . . ."
"One, Two, Three, Four . . ."

We begin again, and then 10 minutes later I get a jolt.
Vision exploding, eyes spewing sparks
Arm twitching with voltage nerve terror
We announce we are taking a break. We hit the back door.

I woke up to the beat, Amarillo, Saturday
To hot rod, Bar-B-Q, Charlie's bar and hamburger mansion
Played wild to 2-steppers and ranch hands until retreat
To untamed outskirts of Route 66 and hoarse windy dreams

Sunday I rose in the afternoon and drove around memories
Recollections of childhood powerful and mystic
With clarity magic and reflective like glass
Like following subconscious sense of direction

Streets and alleys come alive again
In parts of town, dilapidated with decay
When certain veins of the memory are tapped
Springs of clear water erupt to the surface

Lubbock appeals to the sinuses of the mind
And to the allergies of the spirit
The eye sees horizons when none are near
The breath gropes for air in the sparkling dust

Feet feel for wheel when none are there
Receipts are a dime a dozen but business is bad
The fraternities chatter and the bar glasses clatter
But the rule of the cruel is dizziness

Got a cold in my nose and turned in my taxes
Ate a submarine thinkin' bout twin saxes
That played in my brain while I ate the guacamole
My boots got no shine but Lord, are they Holy

Lubbock Rox afternoon set-up
Night brings blown fuse and smoking amp
I am reminded of Lubbock's apathy, want to return to
    London . . .
Some Vickie follows me around all night

Friday, I took my semiannual state of affairs tour
On a bicycle cruising Lubbock suburbs
I saw no other people on sidewalks, in yards, nowhere
To unconsciously circumvent the vastness of the prairie

Perhaps loneliness prefers to be inside with itself
I rode 20 miles before I was satisfied
I love to bicycle in Lubbock, there's no uphill
The wind is the biggest cliff there

I went to see Jerry Jeff and jammed till late
And talked in his wonderful nonsensical tone
I rode bicycle again the next day to Buddy Holly Park
Looking for a site for Tornado Jam

To TV's, again, I went after midnight
Always attracted to nightlife and danger
And my friends, Black Charlie, Shallowater Slim, Joe Murphy
Incandescent lights on green felt, neon on red Naugahyde

The clack of the balls, 8 in the side, the gleam in an eye
The cheap bright clothes, imitation snake and shark,
Shiny hair, patent leather and rhinestone gleams on Joe
    Murphy
Cooking pork chop sandwiches on white bread w/red
    hotsauce . . .

Sunday I sat in a nylon-webbed lawn chair with friends
And basked in the aroma of outside cooking
The day was clear and windy
And the sunlight was like New Mexico, sharp and revealing

Cadillac Mountain on the coast of Maine
Is the first point that the sun touches America each morn
And that's about the time I get home each night.
Sharon said leave; my guitar life-style does not suit her

Came the next day and got my stuff
I'm scatter'd to many winds. Mobile home gone to rust
My country house empty, covered in dust, belongings in boxes
Haven't unpacked from England, now packing again for
    Austin.

I talked to the parks department, silly details about future jam
They say the city's upset

ONE FUSE OF A SUMMER

Thinking we want to conjure up a cyclone. C'mon boys,
This ain't no fountain, it's the sea herself.

I rented a car and got the hell out, picked up Sharon first,
She had cooled down and drove that lonesome road to austin.
We cooked out with the help of headlights
And on to Austin motel in a driving hurricane, 3:30 A.M.

I woke up to a ringing phone in a red room
Motel livin' is the life I lead. They say sound check off.
Chinese restaurant next door to Antone's loud music policy.
Jammed with angelic Angela, white queen of blues.

    Another play day, walk on glass
    Play late night to the shakin' ass
    Take this party to the lawyer's house
    And press our luck on what the law allows.

Sharon leaves mad feigning hurtness
I dont know why I hang around, or why she does
She needs more security and routine than I can give.
Singing, "All you need that I ain't got, is a little routine"

Back on the road, whew, finally, after a day off
Riding with Jesse talking dissatisfaction with band crew
Nothing works, amps, guitars. The band is slow onstage,
Sloppy dressed, thinking of itself as an endless bar band.

I dreamed I was walking between buildings on campus
I notice gun-turrets on tops of buildings
A biplane dives and the students spray it with white powder
I realize it's all a joke.

BONFIRE OF ROADMAPS

The pilot barely misses the tall bell tower
And stalls after a hard turn and clunks down to the ground
A couple of girls fall out giggling. One takes me by the arm
We walked, she talked, I was deep in thought.

I dreamed Chinese sex and delicate weave of carpets
Jesse sat in one room grinning with peroxide hair
One girl took me in a room running her fingers through my
    hair
And said, "I'll show you how it's done."

I rode a bicycle around Lubbock shopping for binoculars
We played with the Planets at the Cotton Club
Saw Gene Glasscock fresh out of Houston drunk charge jail.
He slipping back into pre-prison pattern

ONE FUSE OF A SUMMER

Saw fire 3 A.M. in small wooden alley 2-story
Silhouettes of firemen spraying orange water
Against blue violet sky. The full moon argues
With flashing lights and people crying

Another Cotton Club night berserk and Jesse said he quit
And I said I quit then did an encore
When the stage beckons, I cannot refuse
I didn't blame Sharon when she kicked me out at dawn

I met with the Mayor of Lubbock to talk Tornado Jam
He was cordial and serious, owns a TV station and is divorced
I felt like a seagull on ice, I was not the right person
To represent myself in these concrete matters

We arrange for a stage, P.A., lights, etc.
And figure how to pay for it or else skip town
That night we go to TV's. Sharon finds me like a bloodhound.
Silence like ice. I'm always in jail.

Johnny Green arrives from England with wife Lindy
Like a breath of fresh air straight from Clash tour
At dinner we discuss news from both sides of Atlantic
Hell fire, let's go, I'm bustin loose

Johnny finds the Coldwater cowboys amusing
As well as void of familiar personality.
Will his sense of adventure justify his culture shock?
Tune in later for more . . .

Coldwater again. Johnny asks why we play here
There is no excitement, he says
Everyone sitting on their fucking asses
I agree, by cracky! Wake up! Start your engines!

The big day of the Tornado Jam and I feel like shit
My eye and throat are infected and swollen shut.
A pain rips like a power saw from my jaw to my temple
The crowd seems unreal, aquarium like.

I recoup for a few days, my eyes very bad.
Friday we go to Palo Duro Canyon with Johnny and Lindy.
This landscape must look like the moon to them.
Farm road 400 plowed and barren

Johnny admires the TV dinner packages at gro store in
    Plainview
Lindy looks for English tea and finds Lipton's
We arrive in the canyon at sundown,
Build a fire, and then watch TV like true gypsies.

We woke to the river and climbed a red mesa
Me and Johnny walk to the store and buy a Winston radio
Back at camp, we battle another camper's loud radio
With xtra loud rockabilly and reggae

A storm approaches over the canyon wall
The rains wail and our van rocks violently
We sleep rocking like crazy
And pray for low water not holding our breath

Sunday we go to the drags, outskirts Amarillo
Hot rods and Modifieds lined up for miles
Super stocks roar down the quarter-mile mouths open
Dragsters explode in terrifying smoke and decibel scream

The asphalt melts leaving the smell of nitro and burning
    rubber
Six seconds later the crowd gasps as the monster smashes 240
    mph
I feel empathy as the drivers tear down.
We drive to the Cadillac graveyard and shoot it full of holes.

ONE FUSE OF A SUMMER   103

I dream Mario Andretti tells me performers have a need for
    speed
Some find it in women, some in danger.
I'm talking long distance to a parachutist whose chute won't
    open
"I hope you ain't calling collect," he says, "Reverse the
    charges."

Goddamn Dust! I was born in It, swam in It,
Swept in It, mowed and moved in It.
I've cried in It and woke with mud stains on my pillow.
I've resisted the draft, scattered wild seeds, and attended
    funerals
    in It

I've run with It and against It,
Swallowed acres of It, fought It and flowed with It.
My wise conclusion is only; let It blow! Let It blow!
Blow you goddamn dust, blow!

Driving to Big Spring in a dust storm headwind
The dust devils carve a funnel out of a blanched horizon
We come upon Big Spring scattered in an arid gulch
And looked for the band in the rodeo arena

We play 2-steps and waltzes till the cows come home
And drink beer from a coffin. Soooie!
Later went to a party at an oil mansion of Gary and Ann
Woke on their floor in a great white room

After searching endless halls, I found Jacky in a Japanese room
Face down on a rug that had pressed oriental markings into his
    face.
We gave up waiting on Gary's plane and drove on to Kerrville
Jacky talked about his trunk full of T-shirts he would soon sell

The Kerrville folk music scene always made me antsy
Good ol boys talkin' aesthetics and then vanishing at pay time
A big rain came 3 songs into our set. "Go home," said
    promoter.
We kept playing in the monsoon rain, shouting with glee . . .

I looked around to find myself in a sweaty mobile home.
A blistering Mexican morning in the Kerrville sun.
I called to find that the promoter had shortchanged us
And that Jacky had got drunk and given away all the T-shirts.

Guy and Susanna took me under their wing. We hi-balled to
    town.
Ate Mexican food. Saw a turtle explode.
I dreamed rain under the blue sheets and black birds spoke
Short sentences disguised as blinking neon-cafe signs.

We go see wizard Guy Juke's pastel angles.
He assures me we live in a very square world
His flying weasel takes snapshots with a micro instamatic
His heart is pyramid and his tones are the sawblade and
    cardboard.

We are lucky to be so emancipated; life is too short to get a job
The sweet experience that we carry inside of us
Among friends who create with passion from the heart
Is more precious than any of the *Great American Promises*

This nectar we carry with us till death
As we travel wild and fight the headwinds
Our amigos understand, just like the pale ones before us
In smoky Paris, foggy San Fran, renaissance Italy or beat NYC

Austin is a lusty village, divided by a cool snaky river.
Music is strummed on the vines that sway with the current

And the current powers the steamy clubs
Where the sounds pour out the windows like dragonflies

I didn't feel like leaving but had 1200 miles to make
So I bid good-bye to the carefree south
And packed my tatter'd bag and dusted off my boots
I didn't look back, purely out of habit

I flew first to Lubbock to console my mother
Her hate for her doctor had grown from dependence
If she had a gun, she swore she'd shoot him
I did not offer her the use of mine

Sharon took me to the airport where the jackrabbits played
I kissed her goodbye and walked down the ramp
O sad Lubbock, o fort of my sorrow
Smeared like a smudge on a patchwork quilt

Minneapolis glowed orange on a cool spring night
I rented a Chevy and drove to the Caboose
Where Vasser Clements played his blue electric violin
The shrill notes aroused a frenzy of bats

I met the band in the morning for coffee and eggs
The Fair Oaks motel, somehow was still there
I walked through the park and peeked in the museum
Where the guard looked me over by the cold stone wall

We drove to the venue, miles out of town
To a hockey rink closed for the summer
They had closed off the floor, a web of pipes
It felt like the set for a science fiction massacre

I realized that the audience was all behind glass
Like a dream that I'd had long, long ago
Designed as protection from hockey pucks and missiles
Now stands as a shield to restrict interaction

BONFIRE OF ROADMAPS

I remembered the dream of the South Plains Fair
I was in a band in a booth on the midway
As throngs passed by they stared with blank faces
When I woke I swore it would never happen again

We drove the next day to the city of the north, Duluth
Where the black ore poured through the middle of town
The Crickets played well but Waylon was hoarse
He slipped out across the drawbridge and skipped silently
    away

Johnny Green had long dreamed of the Wyoming Devils Tower
We took I-90 cross the plains of Dakota
Hundreds of miles on a great western detour
On the trail of tears with a case of Budweiser

Taco-up at Worthington, gas-up at the C.B. Burger
And follow the signs to Wall Drug, The Reptile Gardens
The 3P's is open (pizza, pinball, and pool)
Where Elvis vibrates the jukebox alive

We sleep like fools in a plastic motel
Surrounded by fossils and the token TV
The bed never stops, it rocks all night
With highway stripes strobing, forever cross the ceiling

Up in the morn for tea at Wall Drug
We met motel Richard for a drive through the Badlands
Scenic erosion, an X-ray of time, a cavern with no ceiling
A feeling that time had lured us like fish

Rapid City came quick and the Black Hills followed
Johnny now drives like a man possessed
A stop for coffee at the Close Encounters Coffee Shop
And on to the mountain made famous by a movie

Devils Tower was created by a 500 ft. Grizzly
So says the legend of the Black Hills Sioux
We could see it for miles, then disappearing for miles
Then appearing again, staggeringly monumental

Johnny took pictures by the U-Haul trailer
The band stayed in the Budget Rent-A-Van
And the coon-tail swayed on the radio antenna
Merle Haggard sang of prison on the reservation radio

Nighttime found us in Deadwood Gulch
Drinking beer at the Coyote cafe-bar
Wild Bill and Calamity Jane followed the Chinese gold rush
And Poker Alice cleaned up in the wake

No balls here now, just a roadside attraction
Though many sit gloating in the after-light, drunk
TV has made us a foolish race of actors
Trying vicariously to approximate the legend

Our battered bodies climb back in to the ever-rattling van
Past the Swiss Lake at dusk and on to Mount Rushmore

We catch just the nose of George Washington
As the park shuts down the lights for the night

After much yelling in protest, we secede from the Union
And scream out of the hills and off to Cheyenne
Stopping for burgers at the Sunrise Truckstop
Worn to the core like the fools that we were

To a poor boy from Lubbock, a band means freedom
A way of escape, a ticket to ride
So ride we did, next gig, Amarillo
We took the long way thru Colorado and New Mexico

Pack up after Amarillo show for 2 A.M. drive to Lubbock
I argue with crew; I'm at the end of my rope
Like horses in a pasture everyone can smell the barn
"Fine," I say, "I'll just ride on the roof!"

And so this tour ends, at least this leg
With a carload of crazy musicians on Highway 87
And me, riding on the roof of the van screaming with glee
On the Amarillo Highway with the wind in my hair . . .

AUSTIN TO DULUTH AND BACK
May thru July 1980

LORD OF THE HIGHWAY

Yor never cling to anything
until you feel a dangger of losing it
By then your ffear
has made3 you weak
ah but lefe is a paradox
as curley once said
step ping down off the bus
Illuminated with Psychodelics
so i'm riting this opening
paragraphh on highway
in the dark
294 mi. to chicago
in a van pulling a horse trailer
full of Elektric
amps, guitars, and drums

there is a light inseide me
that grows bright and dim
Music is what i cling to
at all cost even life?
so its back ont the road
for a two month run
drgggerent city ebvery night
the orange ligh
shines on the intersate

all the angles are much
too straight the green sighs
and the power lines
t\hat web the word
with network intelligence

i breathed the morning air
at the classic mote4l inn
we've jig-sawed
the united states in half
from gulf ao mexico
to lake surperion
dallas, okc,
tqake me back to tulsa
springfield mo, sad promoters,
rapping radio, hot rods
chinese restaurants
and ozark antiques
i yam the world,
i breathe america
the ununderstandable

In st. louis we watched
The Cardinals pau the Seahqwks
In the unroofed stadium
the perspective made me anx
And i looked through the hole
in the bowl and felt the
Universe sucking the lungs
out of my body
And the crowd cheered
and i cried inside
and held back tears
And i reeled in my line
back to the seat whrer
i was now sitting

and looked to the field
where bodies were scatterd

everywhere scattterd
and a red shirted cardinal
was running for his life
chased by 600 lbs.
of pumped-up meat
and steamed potatoes

    I have stumbled on the plains
    stagger'd in the wind
    stood at a crossroad or two
    cried to a river, swept to the sea
    all just to get to you . . .

It's strange the details
you transparently absorb
When you think you'll never
see them again
things like curio shops
that i once despised
now i look on
as curious beauty
Men sell curious things
Ogbjects of survival
that money battles for
and Curpurations
appear to be built upon

We are at the apex
of inflated pride
As a nation
we are adolescents
entering adulthood
Pimplefaced,
drinking Cokes by the billion,
sons and daughters of pioneers,
croouising the drag,
looking for deals,
ttalking trash,
unguilty by reason

of the Christian business work ethic,
the 3piecesuit sellling
what the blue collar will buy
the bold frontier
must market pride
and style to stay alive

We come into chicago
and see the sears bldg
miles away
Mike commented
that jimmy hoffa disappeared
while They were building
this chunk of concrete.
"The jiminy hoffa
memorial exit ramp!"
Jimmy the bump exclaime
Shehicago looks good,
pperfectly clear sunny cool
summer sunday

I'm back in the light
I can see what I'm writing
The Darkness I leave,
In the hollow misspelled words

I walk in the crisp Chicago air with abandon, going
nowhere. I kick a beer can off the curb and am about to
kick a newspaper, my foot freezes as I see on the sidewalk a
weathered photograph. I recognize the person but it takes
me a second to realize who it is. It is me.

I recall that the picture was taken in the back room at
FITZGERALD'S with an accordion on the wall behind me. I
remember the handle of an old adding machine sticking me
in the back while I tried to look "interested," and the room
was full of jabbering people and I remember what the
photographer was wearing. I imagined the photo to look
much different than what I saw there on the sidewalk.

I looked around to see if anyone was watching me look at
my self there on the street. Then I thought, how stupid . . .
but no, it's not. Here I am all alone in one of the biggest
cities in the world and I meet an image of myself blowing
down the street and I need to relate to this stranger inside
my self.

I have never been captured
In a photograph
I have always hidden
Behind a disguise
Or assumed another personality
I am uneasy with the setting
Because I have made it up,
like a dream I once had

I've never been captured at work,
Where I spend
the most of my time,

It's just as well
What a boring picture,
sitting for hours behind a pencil,
gazing distantly
Guitar in hand,
pants unzipped,
hair twisted like medusa,
rubbing out my eyebrows
With nervous thumbnail

After the show we leave
At midnight for Minneapolis

somebody stole
My Virgin de la Guadalupe T-shirt.
I suppose I will lose
Everything on the road
Sooner or later
every night a different city
Years at a time.

last year I lost
All my guitars
And most of my clothes
the year before
I lost my shoes,
My pants and my ass
I have never lost my Spirit
i've misplaced it, dropped it,
Bruised it and hocked it,
but never lost it,
Thank Jesus

I replaced
My Virgin de la Guadalupe T-shirt
Upon repacking
Back home in Austin
The next road trip
Took us through Cleveland
Where this shy painter
Girl asked for my shirt
In return
For her gold St. Christopher.

I said "here honey
Just take the shirt."
She insisted I must have her chain.
She had had a little to drink
And the spirit
Was moving her deeply.
I accepted her gift
Because I knew
She needed to give it.
Sometimes it's harder
To Receive
Than to Give . . .

LORD OF THE HIGHWAY

1987

GULF WAR ONE

The skittish deer
Avoids the moon
When the hunter's breath
Fouls the brush

It rained all through Christmas. It soaked the parched dirt and spilled into the drains and ditches. Something other than moisture was in the wind. It was audible in the buzzing of the airwaves. The clouds had been building for months. A dark sound was emerging. People's faces contorted to the rumbling that seemed to be coming from below.

Sometimes the whole world goes mad, and backslides, wino-like, into its own vicious History. Back to the times of animals beating war drums, yelling a warning, hallucinating that war has a reason and that victory will bring power to the powerless.

Love thine enemy.
"It don't apply here, sonny boy."

Do unto others as you would have them do unto you.
"After what they done to us?"

The words of Jesus lay dead in the mud. Pocked with gashes, sprayed with shrapnel and blood. The words, themselves, victims of vengeance and revenge.

Soldiers never suspect the horrors of war. They are young and immortal, protected by prayers from home. God is on your side, say the men in stripes knowing deep down that violence breeds violence perpetrating it self unto eternity . . .

Old men who have been there, warn them of their folly. Humanity *never learns,* they say and shake their heads. This is the point where this chronicle begins . . .

The Mad Horses of War, I could feel in my chest,
Came riding on Shards of Broken Glass
The walls rumbled as I closed my ears
And the air retreated from the space it once held

Paralyzed robins in leafless trees
Froze with fear as The Wild Herself
Came roaring through the trunks and roots
Then flew when the Tree caught Fire

Damn Sad, Satan, Sardonic, Sadistic
Sodomy and Hussy
The way George Bush said "Sad-Damn"
I studied the name of Tyrant Hussein

This man who has taken the world
By its balls
Will not release his grip
With just a polite request

He wants the kingdom back
That was scattered by Britain 70 years back
By some Lawrence of Arabia, propped up by Power
In the Movie Version and in the Novel

A spiritual man who was born in a world
Where power is absolute, in a tribal world
Where people pray morning, noon and night
A world too spiritual for Democracy

Where moral behavior is written in stone
And questions are not asked of authority
Where there is no second opinion or religion
Where God snows on those who disagree

I flashed backward in time
Leaving London merely months ago
While the Royal Family of Kuwait
Was shaking the sand from their sheets

The airport was crawling
With robots and police
I was searched until I sneezed;
Police, machine guns, stoic, unamused

Once again, I cross that black ocean
On the dawn of a different world
More filled with fear than with expectations
At the schizoid faces of leaders on the brink

Sleep comes easy
At the rock and roll hotel
If you barricade the door
And put a pillow over each ear

I dreamed of two islands
Bobbing in one lake
Spewing each other with volcanic lava
And Gospel music

I rolled over in to another dream
More Primal than the one before
Of times before the Wheel
In the days of flint and Fire

Back to the Times when tar pits were ablaze
Fed by War-drums, flesh covered
Hypnotic Tattoos beat day and night
To the Mystic Order of Midget Spirits

When I woke, it was dark
My head in a vice
I called to the lobby
To get the time

I walked in a drizzle
To the Neon Cinema
To sit with Bertolucci
Under his Sweltering Sky

I stopped by the newsstand
Ego hungry, needing Media
And bought only the rags
That proclaimed self reviews

How strange I felt
To see pressed in ink
My other self, the performer,
The fool, the Broadcaster of Myth

Back out on the streets
In a razor blade wind
The buildings looked tilted
With blurred street light

My ears began to ring
The air had become thick as a quilt

The city stopped like an animal, listening
Motion and sound turned black and close

A dog-pitched scream inside my head
Traveled outward, snaking through the streets
Then chirped bat-like from the rooftops
Wilting tree limbs and power wires

The very soul of London trembled
With the memory of Blood for Peace
The long sleeping Gargoyles awaken, hissing
Above the mist in my twisted hair

Back at the hotel all suspicions confirmed
The TV ablaze with Saliva and Adrenaline
Iraq has been attacked
The Carrions of War block out the Sun

I watch and I watch
Maybe it's only a plug for Hollywood
Maybe Orson Wells has been reincarnated
And holding up a mirror to Humanity

I fall asleep to see if I am dreaming
Tossing in Vision filled with Vultures
I woke in my clothes, drenched in sweat
The TV belching balls of white fire

The phone is chirping, my cab is waiting
As are the cameras at the Mexican Cantina
Stillness is rare; there is no relief
In the organized chaos of London Town

I film a song, scarf down a taco
Jump in a cab, roll down the windows,
In the lobby of the Columbia sat Pat the Misplaced
Wandering Air Force Cowboy Punk

We went for Indian food
Vindaloo, Dansak and Madras
Red peppers were steaming out our ears
As we panted like dogs between conversations

The band arrived on Thursday
White as ragged ghosts
The War had started while over the Atlantic
But remained unannounced till the taxi at Heathrow

Tony the Driver is already packing
Rental amps and Guitars chosen to ride
The Volkswagen Tour Bus is ready to ride
But needs a new pair of windshield wipers

So off we go on what should be
a tour like any other
But a certain melancholy is riding with us
Something we do not talk about

When a musician dares to explore
New lands, territories uncharted
It is an act of bravery, self-confidence to signal
A method to hurdle new challenge

for sometime now I've known
That Grissom is leaving.
Johnny Cougar sells many more seats than I
And projects a better profile on videotape

David came from Johnny's town
And watched him rise in the Media's Eyes
Now David has a chance to grab a piece of the spotlight
Not to mention fistfuls of greenbacks

After seven hard years of spanking the Muses
It will be hard to see him go
Many long nights of harmonic bliss
May never again be attained

Musicians who play together in time
Share souls in common
Their music becomes blood
Pumping through a common heart

Music must Change
There is no other condition
When one only relies on replicating old tricks
Musicians will then become Actors

The papers quote President Bush
"The Sands of Time have Run Out"
"The Liberation of Kuwait has begun"
The TV goes in a circle, little to report

Green Scud Missiles ripped through the Phosphor
Of German Televisions filled with Green Snow
Green Streaks through a Green Sky
Hitting Green Targets, Oh God . . .

The Holy War is proclaimed:
"The Mother of All Battles"
"Those who die," shouted Saddam
"Will be assured a place in Heaven."

Sweet Sharon and Little Marie
Far, far away in Sweet Texas
Are immersed in the same images
The rest of the World Sees

Tour managers tell us
Many Road Shows have canceled
The airports are Secure; travel not advised
With terrorists Multiplying like chickens

So there you are, and here we go
Not another Euro Tour Nightmare?

I decide that now, more than ever
The people need music, live in the flesh

We leave for Sheffield,
For the Forest of Sherwood
Plastic webs cling to Freeway trees
In slashed, pale February sun

Quaint farms pass our windows
Subdivided by the Ages
Like a handed-down quilt
Repairs to the squares getting ever smaller

We play Sheffield City Hall
The first of a string
Robert Cray's Blues coming through fluorescent lights
Hanging backstage in cafeterias

The news we check each night after show
Israel attacked by Scuds from Iraq
Sand, Death and Jets are buzzwords for today
The Present has no Will to escape

Death-defying reporters report
Missiles passing by the window behind them
Thrill TV viewers like a Televised Circus
This being TV's first "Live War"

All Future Wars will be live, I suspect
From now till the end of Tarnation
Until the natives get bored and the channel they flip
To some Relevant Hollywood Cop Show

Saddam endorses Cable News Network
It's no wonder, as now he well should
Having become The Most Famous Man In The World
Waving his pistol at the altar of Allah

We play the sports arena in Birmingham
The Playhouse in Edinburgh
The Apollo in Manchester, night after night
Watching the War and praying for Peace

A four day run at the Hammersmith Odeon
Coincided with a run of bad news
A Virus checks in to my body's Motel
As double-ought, head to toe, Flu

Singin with a sore throat comes naturally
To a cowboy from the dusty plains
But tonight it's like torture, my voice must crawl
Over coals, thru razor wire to escape

Each night gets worse, Dammit to hell
Carrying me wrapped up in towels
They prop me up with medicinal electricity
And follow my nightmare with follow-spots

I watch the war each night
As if it is the sickness in my own body
In a certain way, war is but a manifestation
Of each person's vulnerability to weakness

Farewell to the Isles,
We're Continental Bound
To Rotterdam's Pirates of Plenty
To sing with descendants of Freewheeling Sailors

To me, they bestow a new funky zealousness,
A respect for the four winds of healing
My strength, returning, my pulse a drum
The blushing front row, see the bulge in my jeans

To the Amsterdam Church
Where the idea of Anarchy
Was born to the Arts, passed on to the Junkies
Now dwells entombed in the tawdry Paradiso

After the show, the opening band,
Funny, their name escapes recollection,
Told us that *they* had a "grand" performance,
And that *we* were "ok" too . . .

The Super Bowl came at 3 A.M.
Live, in roaring color, from the USA
How absurd this glittery event appears
From a European point of view

Then, as if someone tossed a lit cigar
Into a fireworks stand,
The stadium erupts in a brazen attempt
At the ultimate expression of tastelessness

Halftime begins, a few tiptoe out
In case the broadcast became entangled
In some transcontinental Möbius loop
Pulling us all into its vulgar little quagmire

On a tour, a jaunt, an incision
We survey the underbelly of Amsterdam
A lost world of whores and degenerates,
And the lost places known only to them

Knee deep in red light, with a halo of blue
The tattooed lady drinks a glowing drink
And stares, yellow-eyed, at her reflection
In the tinfoil mirror, shattered by time

Down two covered alleys and a tunnel
The air, thick with opium and hashish
A Scene emerges, like Boy's Town in the Fog
The Transvestite Bar, bubbles in burned-out mini-lights

Like a scene in a C-grade Sex-Flick
Trumped-up egos run amuck
By the dawn of the light, they swap once again
In case the Sun-Star blackmails or betrays them

The Towne and Country, back in London,
Is a Time Warp waiting to happen
With enough of the Past to predict the Future
With the future, lost in the Fog

Between the time we go on
And the time that we're done
A message comes from the management to not be surprised
Shane McGowan has drunk all our beer

No bolt from the blue, no surprise, within
His reputation, Shane must maintain
Albert Finney has joined us, we're glad to embrace
His support from the days back in Nashville

Shane takes us to a pub devoid of air
More full of smoke than if it were on fire

People crushed tight, not an eel could slither through
Tighter than the flesh of a cannibal's drum

Halfway in, I felt a panic grab my throat
Turning for the door, my breath tightened
I clawed through the bodies, sweating and panting
Yellow fog covered the windows as I reached for the door

The outside felt like heaven, cold and wet
The gods of Air painted the inside of my lungs
A chilly mist surrounded me, soaking my clothes
As I hailed a warm Black Taxi back to the womb hotel

While I slept, my subconscious prowled
In to the strange history of bouts with Claustrophobia
As if tied together with bobbing buoys
Stretched out in sequence behind a leaky boat . . .

 A fireball the size of a bull
 ripped from my Texas chest
 Remembering a fire from generations ago
 No air, panic, helpless against the cries of the others

 What's taking so long?
 Is that gunfire?
 Where are the children?
 A leather cone awash in flame,
 Smothered in the smell of cooking flesh?

I have to run, I must get away . . .

Generations later in the plains of Texas
Where this memory first came awake
After the railroad had sprawled sea to sea
And brought my forefathers to the suburbs
In a little brick house off Line Avenue
In my grandfather's bedroom
Where the cedar chest smelled like the window facing west.
I remember running from the alley to the garden

And in the backdoor, all thru the house
I was panting from a chase and fell on the bed
The pursuers arrived pillows in hand
Laughing and cruel in childhood abandon
And smothered me white
Till blue for air I fought with animal unconsciousness
Then escaping, screaming among the lilacs
In a dusty crimson Amarillo dusk, desperate
While the adults drank coffee in the kitchen
That they said they should not drink
And ate church cookies by the plateful
Which they said they should not eat

Years later in the Adriatic Sea
Off the coast of Dubrovnik
Once again, within the theme of this audit,
Fighting for my life, found me alone
In an angry rip-tide

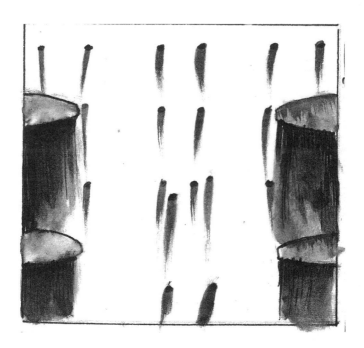

Carried further from land
With each gasping stroke
Away from the rocks of the white walled city
The city retreating with each desperate stroke
Out of breath and out of hope
Until something came to me
And told me to surrender
Unconditionally, with no more struggle
It told me to lay on the water
And drift with the current
And it carried me gently
Three miles south of Dubrovnik
And placed me gently
On the Shore down South
In the direction of Albania and Greece

Decades later in London Town:
I remember that in London for days
I fought this grey suffocation
A desert heat, scourge-like, inside my rib cage
Pressed against cold, clammy England
Where I walked among bomb-threats
Old as Papal Robes and Guinness Stout

When the Desert Shield fell to the sand
And became a Desert Storm
Where I cried for soldiers in a faraway war
On all sides, Universal, flesh and blood
Trapped in the rage of politics and power
Grown Men decorated with ribbons
Pushing plastic weaponry 'round a plywood desert
Estimating whether Allah might approve
Or God might approve
Or Exxon or Shell might disapprove
Armies by the bucketfuls in a rich holy wasteland
With thousands are buried in sandy bunkers
And thousands zipped inside chemical-weapon suits
Hearing the seconds tick between their ears

GULF WAR ONE

Or there, in that basement,
In the gay diplomat's restaurant.
Where I had gone for a quiet dinner
Smeared in fern and grandmotherly
In maroon lace and milk can
Suddenly, I must get away,
From the needle-heat, from the kitchen,
From the whisper of sophisticates, laughing wickedly
Behind the rushes and bamboo shade
The flickering candlelight paints masks on the faces
Faintly familiar to my ancestral memory . . .
Hold me O Father, let me fly!
How could anyone be so civilized?
To endure such binding?

They're carrying me away on a Calvary horse
Smelling of sweat and smoke,
Smoke and sweat, sweat and smoke . . .

Across the ocean where the arrows fly, tra, la, la
Giving birth is kin to watching die, tra, la, la, la, la, la,
    laaaaaahh . . .

GULF WAR TOUR
Winter 1991

JIM BEAM

I would've called you delirious
If you ever told me that someday
My vices would be paying my bills
And pulling me out of a government tar pit

As much energy as I have put into Whiskey and Tobacco
It's a fluke and a half for Whiskey to pay me back
Although in the case of me and Nicky
It may be too late for compensation

Her ghost tracks me everywhere,
Rides in the seat next to me
Crawls in the lining of my jacket
And spirals around my spine in the moonlight

But I've learned to keep her in a cage,
To spit at sidewalk cracks when she beckons
And to keep her at bay with a cheap bullwhip
When she tries to blow smoke in my ear

Back in the tank, Boys!
And load them Howitzers!
Lets go to the Music Zone
Where wild dogs howl when the sun goes down!

And so it's back on the road
I'm prepared for a Wild and Rowdy Tour
Where I come from, Whiskey is like the Ultimate Fuel
Kick Ass Juice, Gunnin' for Tomorrow's Sun

But me and Whiskey parted ways
When Whiskey put a gun to my head
And demanded my Soul in small bills in a brown paper bag
With which he fled, laughing, down the alley

But I came to my senses and entertained the chase
Running for my life like an escapee
I caught up with him on 6th street and Red River
Where he was bargaining with a Beaumont Prostitute . . .

The first night was OK, Everybody was hot
We bled the crowd for an encore but wished,
Wished to hell we were back in Texas
Where people Whooped, and Holler'd, unselfconsciously

Miami is an Honest-to-God Never, Never Land
Never thinkin' about tomorrow till the money runs out
Never worry about nothin' 'cept that your hair looks good
And Never go to bed till all resources are exhausted

The world has need for Babylonian Cities like this
So that Babylon People have a place to go
Hedonism is an Art Form in that it pays for Art
And Art follows Babylon like a Wounded Wolf

Miami Beach is bronze and white and Deco
With silicon enough to float a Cruise ship
It has more of everything that I find meaningless,
Than anywhere else on earth. Maybe I should move?

In Orlando the crowd sits down
Can't they see we're standing up?

And who is this Tuxedo'd man, tanned, clown smile?
Where have I avoided him before?

Downtown Charlotte, shrewdly economically segregated
Has the *HAVES* rooting around in air conditioned caves
Well Lit, Well Policed, Stocked and Out-of-Sight
Of the *HAVE-NOTS* who hold on to the streets

I was Panhandled six times in one block
And gave to them all, Thank God
And as the sky turned pink and gold
The disenchanted faces took on the tint of flame

If dreams are free on Goddam TV
Then why are the Free so Poor?
Where did the Prophets go? Madison Ave?
And why did they abandon their Children?

Everything at the gig was Peppermint and White Bread
That is until our band began to play
Pained expressions and hands over ears dominated
The side of the room where the Guitar pointed

Do I attract Psychotics naturally
Or is it that music brings out the psycho in people
Lucinda feels it too, the Prowlers, the Sycophants
In a race with sanity, stalk our skinny white asses

I watch the reflection of a silver jet
Fly into the golden windows of a glass building
Later that night I drew it on the table at the restaurant
And spilled wine in the plates of our Sponsors

The Corporate Crew is a bunch of Pussies
They talk constantly behind the Musicians Backs
Afraid of the Corporation, Careful of the consequences
It's just a job to them, to us it's real life.

The pleasures of life in a 4-piece band
Flat tire at 70 mph led to breakfast in a Georgia Truck stop
Lizard-Eyed truckers watched the Rock Band eat
Biscuits and gravy with grits and grease

Grissom watched the Kentucky Derby in the bus
In the alley behind our future Venue
I stroll downtown Nashville to see if I remember
The face of the poet dishwasher who once was King

John Prine was impressed with the Jim Beam Tour
"I've tried for years to be sponsored by Whiskey"
"But the Big Boys just run the other way"
"Besides, Jameson's is my brand of choice."

I sorta lost it in Louisville
Swearing to myself to stay in
But when Louisville Bill wanted to bet on Pool
I packed up my stick and headed to town

As the night wore on, I lost all composure
I swore and swung and bragged out loud
I won and lost and won some more
Sincere apologies to those who suffered

To those who have kept me goin'
With kindness and respect
You have filled my life with sweetness
And I will attempt to fill yours in return

Night after night of bad graffiti
Scrawled on the backstage walls of Clubland
Adolescent yelps like those of a puppy
Hit by a sportscar on Life's Cruel Interstate

I'm tired of yelling over the top of a loud band
Fighting to climb the chain link fence

Kicking the audience in the collective groin
Making them bleed with Volume Ego

Energy given is energy received
But it must be given from the heart
For false energy is a Quagmire
Buzzing with flies who are licking their chops

I look into the eyes of the audience in the dark
And I see a longing for emotional fulfillment
Not to be confused with intellectual awareness
Like concepts, which turn good men into Critics

Writing Theater on the Run is a strange way to work
On Fax machines and from city to city
A Dustbowl life about a West Texas Hooker
Written in airplanes and taxis

And so I abandoned this Journalog as we kept up a roll
Through Columbus, Pittsburg, Alexandria, Virginia Beach,
Richmond, Philadelphia, Northampton,
New York City and Boston and probably more . . .

DUBLIN

Back tracking through history, Boston to Dublin
Is a Study in Culture, turned wrong-side-out
Boston is bigger, richer, fatter, but somewhere along the way
Lost its Humor, Self-esteem, Morality and Unity

So we land again in the land of "Tears and Cheer"
And walk the dark streets we have walked before
Zigzagged the side streets, zipper'd down Grafton
And like a sewing needle, threaded the bars bottom to top

I sleep a restless, jetlagged sleep
Tossing and turning giving my pillow a pounding
I wake too early, not a swallow has stirred
Not an engine has turned nor coffee pot blossomed

I walk in the dawn, James Joyce by my side
Telling me lyrics to the songs he is writing
I kick a tin can and wake up the neighbors
Who find us at Bewley's over coffee and crumbs

In the boxing arena we brace
For the real test of time
Will we slug it out with ghosts or will
The Spirits of the Living dance in the Aisles?

Springsteen shows up, like a saint in black leather
Mere minutes before Showtime
We invite him to join us, to wing it with abandon
Which he rips through the finale to the glee of the Irish

We go out on the town to Bono's brother's Joint
Bruce invites me to his show at the football fields
I accept with grace and prepare to abandon
My flight the next morning to Zurich

A sea of Irish, all primed-up on Guinness
Await the big show with reserve and respect
I work thru the harmonies backstage with the band
Bruce conducting attitude with bearing

The first chord is struck and the fire is lit
With a roar enormous like Gaelic heart
Music turned energy in harmonic wedding
As Bruce steers his chariot stampeding

He calls me to the stage, I walk proudly
An the band responds with verve
I feel the blood gush through my heart
When the black girls sing "Would You Settle For Love!"

The song seems to end before it begins
I could have sung until the sun came up
Bruce calls me back with the Killer Jerry Lee
A fantasy of childhood is fulfilled

After the show, we head back downtown
To broadcast our built up reserve
To a dinner at a dance hall where the well-heel'd stumble
And swing from fake chandeliers

As all things must end, something else must begin
Though often it is too soon for reason
So I bid farewell to my New Jersey Amigos
Terry the Dark Side, Bon Jovi and Bruce

In Kandersteg wait Sharon and Marie and Mark
Like a warm wind blown fresh from the South
I breathe easy. How could I be so blessed?
After a hard journey to be greeted with Love . . .

We walk the trail 5 miles up the mountain
To an unlikely Café by a tranquil Alpen lake

JIM BEAM   137

Across the water we watch in disbelief
As an Avalanche cracks and tumbles to the water

It's an Ashi Masquerade, at the Festival by Frutigan
Swiss Cowboys with Chaps from Peru
They do the John Wayne Strut with one eyebrow cocked
As they trip over their Lassos and Bootstraps.

Johnny Cash and Crew hold down the Hotel
Having lunch with June and Tom Russell
When the paparazzi arrive Johnny nods to June
"Time to make a break for our lives!"

The Photographers anticipate their pathway
And crowd the door as the elevator arrives
When Johnny gets on, the circle does tighten
He holds out his hand and proclaims, simply, "Stop!"

The Reporters do stop, within the width of a dime
Johnny announces, "Five minutes, boys, I'll be back down"
Then says to Tom and June, as the elevator doors shut,
"In about a Million Years"

EUROPE TO PHILADELPHIA

I can't shake the Jet-Lag, the Clock's got me duped
Terry swerves into the airport, like a Manhattan dishrag
I'm hangin' on to the arm rest, Shotgun, God
Sharon's in the middle making nervous reply

Old friends all together in a big jet plane
Raised from the same dirt, familiar Sense of Humor
Irony, satire, intellectual sarcasm, not low or mean
Just a play on words and a desire for freedom

We rehearsed the ragged cast upstairs, 3 flights
The smile of familiar faces is a godsend
I don't have to travel for ten whole days
I'm at home away from home, who would'a thunk it?

BROOKLYN TO THE JERSEY SHORE

Crescent evening moon over the red bricks of Brooklyn
And beyond, the walls of Downtown Manhattan
Silhouetted against the golden Western Sky
Thru the arches of the Brooklyn Bridge
Visions of Whitman who sang this carousel
And Visions of the Immigrants who built it
The car races over nails and potholes
The driver wills it forcefully to its destination
Winding by factories and facades
Over the Verrazano Narrows on a Dangling bridge
Driving the streets of Asbury Park
With the Boss in a Coffee-colored Cadillac
I could hear the Doors thru 30 years of memory
Escaping the Moroccan windows of the Convention Center
The teenagers drink beer by the Merry-Go-Round
The Merry-Go-Round that was sold to pay what was owed
To the Landlords who bought farmers' farms
And chopped them into plots, calling them "Estates"
They then carved streets and chopped down the trees
And in honor of the missing trees, they named the streets after
    them
And planted exotic trees from China and Australia
They put up walls and fences, hence tripling the pricetag . . .

Meeting for sound check at Madison Sq Garden
With Bruce to benefit the Kristen Carr Foundation
Sitting backstage, tuning my guitar
In walks Tulley, my Mi'kmaq amigo from New Brunswick
He laughed in a way that defied reason
And told me the story of his journey from the North
And when he got to the City, he asked a homeless musician
    for directions
Which led him through the tangled streets to this back
    room . . .

JIM BEAM TO JERSEY
Summer 1993

LAREDO EAST AND WEST

Whirlwind of Whirlwinds,
The Road is a Spiral
From Route 66 to the Pyramids at Cairo
Ever Teasing, ever Deceiving,
Equal in Balance between arriving and leaving

It beckons the drunken Dreamer to follow
Seduction Slick in Asphalt Manifest-o
Pot-holed and rooster-crowed,
The Exit can't wait, for the Road to corrode

The Red-Eyed Mystic Plows Future Forth
Tied to Bonds that Babel in Tongue
Pinpricked, Cow-licked, the Future is Young
Moist with tears, stained with coffee,
Mixed with diesel and blood

The rodeo Cowboy with his Saddle in the Back
A double cab pickup, no gun in his rack
He's secure in insecurity, Death tracks his every breath
The Bedouin with his empire of sand

The poet, the dreamer, on a mission from God
City to City, Berg made of Clod . . .

The Road always waits, patient as Sky
Sun on one end, moon up on High
The on ramp and the off ramp
Like a snake with a mouth at each end
The freeway ain't free, No Sir-Eee
It's but a charge account

We imagine a destination,
We concede to a one night stand

Anticipation lets us graze in Elysian Fields
But Mortality has plotted us a Brand New Route
And even changed the Maps
In the glove box.

The majestic interstate,
Eisenhower's grand defense plan,
Stitched together this pompous Republic
With mobile targets
To drive the Russkys crazy
Mighty Missiles
Masquerading as Milk Trucks
Sailing the Shimmering Asphalt
From Silo to Shining Silo

Discriminating not
Between the Weighty
And The Weightless
The Empty and the Temptress

The Road gives right-of-way
To Bleeding Desperados
Fleeing their long lost Notion
That freedom is their long lost Ocean
No matter that their rusted Rambler
Broke down in a dusty shamble
Half way between Comfort and Welfare

The Road also lets pass
The Weightless Ones
Angels and Spirits
Wild Wing-ed Messengers
Who traverse the Lace Mesquite
And spiral the Rusty bob-wire
Mounted High on hood
Lighting the Way
Of Weary Truckers
Ticket in hand

Pathway of Miracle-Seekers,
Escape route of Life-Stealers

Highway of intake and exhaust
Artery of life at any cost
The Carburetor, Injector
Sucking air in a panic
Only to blow it out the Tailpipe
Give and Take, donate the Keepsake
You must leave what's left
To the Unknown, and the Unborn
The Road will balance Tomorrow
Uniting the Country Doctor
With the Cry in the Wilderness

Connecting Summer's Harvest
With Autumn's Markets
Thus pollinating Winter's Seed
To give rise to Spring's new leaf

Procession route of the hearse,
To windy burial ground's purse
Where the Weary make one last Journey
From Deathbed to Graveyard
The Road is All, symbolic of Time
Old as Stardust and Vapor
Meandering through the Universe
Where pathways cross and beckon

Where beacons rarely ever reckon
The need for light . . .
So there ya go, Honcho, hasta la bye-bye
I'm off for Los Pecker-Headed Montañas
In my new house on wheels
With a new band of gypsies, freshly healed
Seasoned travelers, all

Thru the BBQ town of Llano,
North to the Caprock
Sweetwater, Roscoe, Snyder,
Post, Slaton, Lubbock

Lloyd joins us after Orlando's pasta
Bidding the Hub City farewell
Sailing sweetly round the loop, when,
Bam! Dammit! A blowout! Hell Fire!
There goes the first night sleep
Now we must barrel straight thru . . .
Why do flat-fixers not carry a jack or a spare?
The same reason that hard travelers
Lie to themselves about their destinations?
Believing Divine Guidance will lead
The Blessed to Wrenchlessness?
Or, the only other reason for a man
In the business of Highway Service,
That he, being of sound mind and body,
Is beyond giving a Rat's Ass . . .

DUSTY DALHART TO CLAYTON S GATEWAY

A falling star severs the night sky
The Horizon responds with no surprise
Leaving a train of sharp glowing cinders
Swaying like a curtain in a Reno casino

I stop on the Roadside
And I gawk in reverence
I can smell the high
New Mexican plain,

The faint ponderosa
I see the tiny lights
Of little Raton,
Ratoncito,
The little mouse that
has nibbled
A high mountain pass
Through the Brave
Rockies of Colorado
Just wide enough
For a river of
Lowriders
To spill through the
Cowboy Streets
Of Old Trinidad

I pass the torch to Ray
Charles
As dawn lights up the
Mesa
And drift into rude
Orange Sleep
As the Fireball sears
away the mountain
mist

By Pueblo I'm rocking inside a 5-ton Womb
Lulled by the Unpredictable
The texture of Wind and Road
Tossing one way with the gnashing of teeth
Vibrating across a series of bumps
Then deeper and deeper, Enough Already!
Into the Chaos of Sweet Organic Motion

Tonight we play by a Singing Mountain Brook
That rushes with the flow until we turn Upstream
Our flustered limbs stretch for The Tempo
I struggle against rhythms,
My body, out of sync
A thousand miles in a thousand minutes

Has lagged My Ragged Ass out
I kick the mic stand off the stage
I throw harmonicas into The River
I pour 100 proof whiskey into the Monitors
I light my guitar with the flames from my clothes
And leap into the audience like werewolf
The PA explodes with horrific wind
Erupting an avalanche of boulders
People scatter, some crushed in the mud,
Screaming with trembling white tongues
A wall of mud pushes the pool tables
Majestically out the back windows of the burning bar
All lights blow at once as the transformer dissolves
Hari-kari like, in a shower of comet-shaped sparks
And then suddenly, too suddenly,
All movement stops,
Save the sway of the Pines

I think to myself,
Kickin' off a tour with a Flourish, eh?
I fall back, in a rubber lawn chair,
Eyes closed, frozen in the Red Mud of Time
When I open them again, the Dust has settled
Orion peeks out into the night cautiously,
Phone in hand . . .

I relax after the show in a Cosmic Barnyard,
Where baby goats and peacocks
Dance a Colorado Tango
Each ridden by an ugly little gnome a foot tall
Smug in black leather, smoking cigars
Strutting proudly in the mountain air
Past blooming hollyhock
Wilting under Altitude stress
The silence is cold and Empty
Leading me to return to Hotel Neverland,
Where no one ever speaks
Not even the Ghosts
Of Rooms Undone.

OFF TO WEARY FATHER DENVER

Pawn Shop capitol of the Vortex Mother
To limp downtown in a beat-up cab
At the recommendation of the motel maid
The Festival of Fat is in full swing,
Americans at their Leisure
Hot Dog in mouth, Hamburger in hand,
With a 64 oz. Coke, 3 fat kids
And a skinny anemic wife
Chain-smoking Camel Ultra Lites
In purple and pink Big Logo Polyester
Jogging suit strutting Nike running shoes
Made with 6 kinds of Black and White Rubber
Baby in a backpack, huge bag of diapers
As if Baby will pee a Goldfish Pond
Daddy looking tired, wishes he were home
In front of Divine Television
Drinking 6 packs of Busch
Watching the Broncos whoop the Redskins
Topped off with a cozy game of "Mortal Combat"
Then "Doom," then Leno after Valium . . .

Victorian Denver once had it all,
Blessed Mt. Prairie
Forget about her Gargoyles and Airports
She had a Figure and a Suntan
And a trainload of Daddy's Money
But she got a little greedy and bet on Yankee Bankers
Puttin' Red Hotels on Park Place
While old time settlers suffered
And gathered in droves on desperate avenues,
Listening to America's erratic heartbeat
Some living, some dying,
Some turning rubble into art
Inventing new music and language of the beat
Broadcasting it by hand from coast to changing coast

And so we played on Jukebox Street
We played until the dancers twirled

Then slept in tired Motel Rooms
With shower tile on bedroom walls
I dreamed of Lubbock's dreary High School Gym
The dreaded cinder-block and steel Cyanide-o-torium
Where Pom-Pom girls screamed from their breasts
And had hard and sticky hair
They smelled of Lilac and Lavender
And wore make-up made of horses hooves
I dreamed Coach Ma-hawk-a was givin' me licks
With a Flaming Hollow-Point Paddle
With the cheerleaders cheering him on,
Their makeup, their hair melting down their faces . . .

We woke in a haze, in a mile-high smog
And searched the Once Rocky Mountains
For signs of high society, money, models and lawyers
And found them all, dreaming by the pool
At ten-thousand-some-odd feet

ANTI-GRAVITY SUCKED US TO THE TOP OF SNOWMASS

To Thin and Glorified Air
We watched as stagehands waited out the storm
Then slid down Rainbow's Edge
As the most glorious cloud EVER
Passed over the Mountain of Music
I squinted my eyes and sighed,
And hurt inside for someone to share this with
Then realizing that I had a choice
And chose the high and lonely road
Took pleasure in my freedom
And wished I had a shotgun
To give that rainbow a slightly ragged edge . . .

I saw old friends with red cheeks
Sitting on Willie's bus in a cloud of hemp
I had seen Tina Ruby but twice since the days of "Stomp"
We reminisced our gypsy days in the Euro-zone Theater
Happy for the experiences but glad they ended when they did

When the last song played I drifted in to the little village
Where I was attracted to the pool table
Much like a moth to fluorescent lights
And played with three bad lookin' hombres
Who hated to lose, especially to out-of-towners
A drunk woman was stirring up static
And the static was clinging to me
Los Malos were steaming in their own sweaty stew
Their eyes swam in quicksand sinking around me
The drunk girl grabbed their eight ball
In the middle of a shot and the room got quiet
"Damn," I thought "I've had enough"
Alcohol is stronger than the Will of Man
So I willed myself outside into the cool night,
She came cryin' round the corner
"They kicked me out" she screamed
"Like a common lowdown drunk"
I tried to convince her that they were right
And to go back in and drink some more

But she ranted and raved,
And foamed at the Mouth
And followed me closely
To a party in Jesse's room
Where I gave her the key to our spare room

And pardoned my self and slipped away
Down the hallway to freedom
I tossed and turned in a restless sleep
Dreaming of a Wild Woman Circus
Where the Clowns had all rebelled,
They dressed in black leather
Trying their best to be self-consciously un-funny

I danced to the idling bus, glad to be gone . . .
We coasted out of Aspen back to air and to earth
Out across the Plains where my heart did quiver
So long Colorado, adios los montañas

I'll think of you at sea level
When the hurricanes are threatening
And the palm trees are swaying
I was born with a Vision,
I need no more Obstruction
McDonald's for coffee
Diamond Shamrock for fuel
Just turn my ass loose in Jackrabbit Country
Let me roam all day thru Kansas

My thinking commences to reverse
As I yearn for at least one tree
Prairie Madness is Real
Although highly over-amplified

I settle for a weird dinner in Limon
And pay tribute to John Wayne's cowboy posters
He must have stopped here in his day
And waited for his dinner
Then chased a mighty lightning storm
Clean across old Missouri
Stopping for sleep in God knows where
Chasing outlaws in dirty black hats
Who stole some cattle down in Texas
And he found 'em at the Waffle House,
Beat 'em half to death, then ate.

Nashville now at midnight, with its beacon,
The intimidating Bat Tower Building
Glows so familiar it makes me Wonder
Why my life keeps reconnecting
With the powers that do big Business,
To sustain and nurture my family
To Record my wildest moments
And capture my deepest Feelings
Why Nashville, why not Florence,
Atlantis, Rio, Pompeii or Mobile?
Why Nashville for my showing of Jail Life?
The brochure was wrong, the paintings dimly lit

But the snacks were good and the beer was cold,
The talk was loud, the TV lights were bright
The paintings about Nashburg were way in the back
Hidden, where few dared to tread
We must not have controversy here
In the land of Strait and Travis
How ironic, to be in Country Music Headquarters
With an art show about Lost Freedom,
A new album about Lost Love
With a Flamenco-playin' Dutchman from Spain . . .

Anyway, we played our music down by the river
And the night was magic, Lloyd and Jesse wailed
Glenn and Don locked us all in as Teye spun his Gypsy fingers
And an angel came to me in my dreams
And I slept in peace and harmony
And thanked the God of Rambling Fools once more.

I fly back to Austin,
My bones sore and stiff
My first test of touring
Since my crackup in the Spring
In my heart there's still a desert
In the Vacuum I left behind
But I still hang on to the faith
That love will come again
Marie and Sharon wait for me,
Strong, stubborn and brave
Not sure that I have regained my sanity,
But trusting all the same
The first day back I go to the studio
To record with Terry Allen and David Byrne
And set up sessions for later that night
To record a toast to the great Buddy Holly
Wailing away at three A.M.
Oh Boy, yeah boy, sounds like it rocks
But I really won't know till it's mixed
By then we'll be miles away

No turning back, the highway is final
And therein lies my frustration
I have either too much time or too little
Now, I have not even the time to change my clothes
Before my ship sails again to the west,
Sunny Psycho-California, home to anxiety and reverie

LAREDO WEST

La Cienega's clutter'd interface,
Vying for the attention of the Jaded,
Pitching propositions to those who already have One Of Each
Society's twisted fashion gauge
Is it Sheik, Sleek, Slick and Suave?
Where can one go to find it?
Will it still be Modern tomorrow?

We check in to the French hotel on Beverly
Long enuf to splash water in our faces
Then boldly out into the world of The Media;
Radio, Magazines and Cheap Talk, Inc.

Suddenly, without warning, good news is upon us
Amtrak is giving us a train car! HOT damn!
The smell of diesel comes wafting across my Senses
Good news indeed!
It is the way I've liked to travel since childhood
Memories of hearing the dining car's tinkling glasses
With old railroad man, granddaddy Morgan, at my side
Knowing now why he talked like trains
Smelled like trains and lived by the Schedule

We play briefly at the Tower on Sunset,
Where I see old friend Michael Ventura
Thinking how odd that he gave me The Book
Of García Lorca's Gypsy Ballads
During the Flatlander Days
And here in LA, eons later, I am debuting Songs
Inspired by that magic work

Michael is no stranger to odd coincidences, however
Having been inspired in Clarendon and Lubbock
Learning to laugh with the supernatural
At the very second that coincidence becomes Divine
    Guidance

It's on to the Viper Room
I give a call to Bruce, leave a message,
Then a call to La Raj, and hang up during the first ring
There is a strange Void inside me,
I feel she is so close
I cannot see her, the pain that I carry daily
Would be intolerable in my weakness
I prepare for the show with a bath made hotter
Until her memory is melted by lava
I feel pre-show adrenaline invade my body
As I begin to think of songs to perform
Suddenly I'm backstage at the Viper Room
And Bruce and Patty appear

We walk onstage with a Vengeance,
Head high, Los Tres Vatos Malevolantes
The music breaks character and shows another side
When we expose Fire and Beauty
Teye's fingers startle his guitar
Vapors of Desire incinerate in the hot stage lights
Familiar faces appear in the crowd
The Haze surrenders to the Curtains of Touch
Bruce joins us with harmony strong and sure
And we know that we have given our hearts
And the crowd knows as well
These are the moments we live for,
All else is just Highway and Howdy-do
On to Bruce and Patty's for midnight breakfast
The house is lively and the chef is cookin'
Teenage girls are fabricating crossword puzzles
A Holy Order pervades that is manifested
In the Songs they play together
Awareness in accepting the Blessings of the World

The Gifts that God has given to them
In the Form of Children Sleeping
Time for me to sleep as well
Bruce drives me to the hotel, we say adiós
And I roll up in the cool sheets of the Sofitel
Waking to a Film Crew and a Big Ass'd,
Diesel Drinkin' Loco-Motion Machine.

Imagine if every sound you made
Were recorded for others to hear
And every move were filmed for later review?
For the next four days I was sentenced
To a sort of self-inflicted purgatory
Where I would see every movement before It Came
And hear my words before I spoke
I felt Catholic, torn between Mardi Gras and Lent,
Mindful of every fault and shortcoming
Apprehensive of the difference
Between what is Real and what is Image
If the Camera showed Truth
Then Saints would be Movie Stars
Shakespeare would have been a Sunday School Teacher
And James Dean would've sold bibles in Nebraska

We leave the Amtrak Station the next AM
Say so long to Damned Almighty LA
Cameras whirring, the Iron train waking
The sound man catching every breath with his furry mike
CNN right behind with yet another crew,
Circling like a vulture, following the Train Angle
If only they could've seen me in yesteryear,
Sluggin' it out on the freight trains, sleeping under bridges
That was the story, then, not this,
But big deal, that story's gone now,
They are left with this ragged warrior
Limpin' along tellin' lies

We meander up the coast following the Fault
Through huge and troubled mountains

California is a world that was never finished
As if it is undecided on its image of itself
It tosses and turns in its insecurity
And cares not what lay destroyed in its path
Relentless with psychopathic turbulence
California is a stalker who sleeps most of the day
Then prowls at night when the air is cool and seductive,
When the moment is most magical, the music crescendos
And the drugs kick in and orgasm is a squeeze away,
Then California's alter personality appears
Lashing out with a Vengeance,
Fire, Flood, Riot or Earthquake
Reducing all in its path to small insignificant creatures
Waiting in miserable lines waving an insurance claim . . .

Today we trade Southern Tension for Northern Force
Following the great Pacific Ocean on the Coast Starlight
Feeling a tad bit guilty for traveling in such comfort
I'm reminded of my youth as the grandson of a railroad man
Remembering these tracks, traveling with my family
In a more modest, more Western period of time
During the later days of California's Golden Era
After the Goldrush but before the MoneyRush
What magic erupted from this Primordial Landscape!
When California bloomed sweet smells
When Nature was in Balance and Hollywood was Innocent
Before Dirt bikes and Dune Buggies
Before the Redwoods of the North learned about Fear
And whispered in trembling breath at every passing breeze

O Berkeley of Old, Whither the Hell didst thou plow?
Your streets, once bastions of the Ideal
Now are fortified with Surveillance and Security
Violent, emaciated youth parade in mock defiance
Intimidating those who carry the torch for Intellectual
    Emancipation
I realize the traveler sees only the outside of cities
I suspect that a more pacific design is being forged indoors

Where chattering
  networks disassemble
  the global knowledge
Digest as much as they
  can before the
  Scourge sets in
Then weld the pieces
  back together in a
  fleeting, transient
  mosaic
Hounded by Encryption
  or the lack thereof
And that the
  Government will
  secede to the
  Egotistical Idea
That the Right to
  Privacy is separate
  from National
  Security
Or that Telegraph Ave. is
  separate from the
  Web

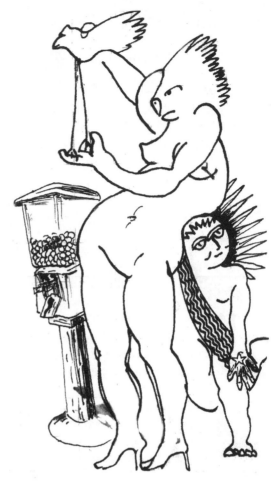

I waved farewell to my
  dear friends, sorry
  they had to remain
As we fought our way
  thru the Telegraph Thicket
And on to the Am-Traks of Unconscious Oakland
There we were told that a gang had tried to sabotage The Train
Having tossed a refrigerator on the tracks
Half full of used syringes and empty Gatorade bottles
Puncturing a hole into the Vital Organs of Our Engine
Thus separating this group of travelers from their Mother
And altering our pre-determined course to Nowhere
This gave me tremendous joy which I had to conceal
So as to not appear to mock those in my company
Who were gravely considering the alternatives

And missed the gorgeous sunset that lit the massive freight
    trains
In a golden glow of Heavenly Light

We said farewell to our camera crew and lovely Trey
And made our way to Sacramento, meeting new faces,
Exploring the Mysterious Universe of Tower,
Where Melody and Rhythm meet Marketing and Power
There catching up with the latest high-jinx of Beavis and
    Butthead,
Our soul mates and supervisors on Matters of Greater
    Importance
Who advise Charles, Steven and Teye to go gamble in Reno
And advise me to do nothing at all
Except observe the wardrobes of corporate employees
And how this relates to nothing at all . . .

In Davis I meet with relatives I have not seen since youth
Idyllic memories of when my father was alive and happy
We exchanged sheepish conversation in the glare of
    fluorescent light
After a record store performance
We traded numbers and said good-bye knowing but not saying
That death has scattered our families to the four winds
Yet we had each created an order from the disarray

The night train sneaks out of the station
I fall asleep immediately to the sway of the tracks
I dream of a golden mountain
Surrounded by orange highway pylons
Forest rangers with white wings
Carrying briefcases leaking water
Wearing headphones with rabbit ear antennas
I woke in a haze to see Mount Shasta
The color of fresh peaches in the morning sun
Like an apparition that connected
The boundaries of my dreams

With the majesty of God's Creation
Instead of beauty stimulating my consciousness
It lulled me back to my dream
Where white square dancers were dancing to Bob Wills
In a freshly yellow-striped parking lot
At the base of a rumbling volcano

The afternoon show in Portland was rocky
Bad store, bad PA, self-centered and mean
But later that night David Lindley shook the Aladdin
His greatness gave me the blues
Which lasted well into the night
I thought about all I have thrown away,
All the wasted nights on the Road
All the unproductive endless Chatter and Clatter
That comes with Hotels and Highways

The Northwest coast was hand-crafted by God
Built just for Adam, then Adam moved to Seattle
To sweep up aluminum shavings at the Jet Plant
Eve stayed in Portland, raising the kids
On pine nuts, wheat grass and dandelions
Home schooling them on Chapra and Sams
Teaching them how to weave
Hula skirts out of wild grass
And how to gather energy from rocks
Stacked in pyramid stacks
With a crystal in the king's chamber,
Obsidian at the pinnacle
And an offering of fresh broccoli scatter'd in a ring
At the base of what will soon force the kids back to school . . .

Adrian called to say that the video was on
And that what you Dream is what you Is
But that the song to film had changed
In the name of possible commercial acceptance
Instead of a flamenco dancer emulating a fighting cock,

Telling the story of Gallo del Cielo
The cameras would follow me
Emulating a wounded soldier
Who lost his camera in the War
Feeling so helpless when the young girl fell
Off an unmarked Stage in the Music Hall
Telling the story of trying to catch a taxi cab in Wichita Falls
Then beating the moon with my fist when I fail
Fleeing across the Rio Grande in a Long Horned Cadillac
To the Sioux nation where I sleep on railroad tracks
Face down in the gravel between the ties
Letting seven trains pass over my body
Thus proving my manhood
In less than four long minutes
Just in time to catch the next bus out of town . . .

LAREDO EAST

Look at the pain that a year has painted onto my face
And the change in the colors that my hungry eyes see
Healing in Motion, absorbing the Agony
Stabbing my bones with each Flaw of the Highway
Like a listless warrior following his Sword
Pain gives some men the wisdom to avoid all pain
In others it inspires them and prods them into battle
Where they run blindfolded,
Shouting into a megaphone, balls in hand
Convincing the Enemy how strong,
Tall and well-armed they are!

No time to unpack, it's off to New York
The Coast is Clear like the voice of Joan Baez
With whom I share a radio show
James McMurtry is there in all his Beatness
Singing a song about Levelland
I feel in another era, like a hillbilly, Transported
New York takes me in her arms and tells me
Close your eyes, it'll be all right in the Morning . . .

For the next two weeks I lay down my pen
I have bounced between Oceans so quickly
That I can only observe from second to second
The colors of Autumn have set the East Coast on Fire
And set my wild mind to Reeling

We passed thru the Graffiti of Pittsburgh
The Birch Streets of Old Alexandria
And dined in the World Café in Philadelphia, PA
We shouted in the Pearl Streets of Northampton
But The Egg of Albany fried our Ass
And took a coat of paint off of the Tioga Ballroom
Up in Portland, Raoul had a fallin' out with Charles
And he let 'em have it, drivin' off into the Muddy Night
Mama Kin danced with Steel Shoes in Bloody Boston
And wouldn't stop until the Cowgirls wrestled Alligators
We were pickin' up steam in each new Joint
The Band was startin' to Sweat,
And the Sweat was startin' to Show

Reeling through the musical hills of sweet Vermont
All pain subsided and I was able to breathe a Slow Sigh
The flaming landscape saturated my spirit
Transforming my eyes into vast nets of ethereal mist
My journey was only beginning, I told myself
A ramblin' man must pursue his harmony
And take refuge in beauty and balance
And when the Sap starts to Flow in the Maples
Then it's damn well time to make Syrup . . .

Burlington is a name I know from the Railroads
I remember catching a Burlington Northern Freight
Having no Idea whether Burlington itself
Was a town, a sweater, or a mountain
The name itself had a kind of Magic,
Like Santa Fe and Rock Island of Old
Gangs of bored teenagers roamed downtown
Each armed with studied nonchalance
Feigning detachment on the Surface

Yet terrified of the Very World just below the Skin
The boys, repositories of dammed up testosterone
And the girls, secretly desperate to be Wanted
Dancing the Eternal Dance of Aggression and Indifference
Not unlike the mating ritual of the Crocodile
Maybe a bit more Dangerous and Deadly

Another drive the next day across the breathtaking hills
Zigzagging from Vermont to Connecticut
Into New London at dark, blowing another tire
Reminding us that we all were beginning to suffer
From a serious case of Severed Valve Stem

The Tioga Ballroom wobbled into Manhattan
Like a frightened Dinosaur into a Tar Pit
Knowing fool well it was eminently out of place
But sensing the presence of fellow creatures
Waded in up to its virtual neck
And shivered in the bog daring God and Good Sense

No sooner than the Sleep was scraped from our Eyes
And the Spiders chased from our Brains
Did we find ourselves on Conan O'Brien
Being Irish, I'm sure he understood the Concept
Of dancing a happy jig in a Stadium full of Cobwebs

And so we present, on National Television,
A story of a Refugee pining for his Lover
A half a World away, in the Back Streets of Laredo
The Singer jumped bail from a Barney Fife jail
To cross the River of Tears and No Return

You don't just leave Manhattan, you escape
Through a series of mazes and passwords
To exit through Spanish Harlem takes nerve
Many men tried and many men failed
To find the bridge to lead them from their failure

We sail out across New Jersey, where the West begins
Headed for Kentucky where they make Jim Beam
The East is heavy with many Gravities of old
Pulling against newer Gravities, Television, Film and Internet
At the Pennsylvania border the restraint is gone
As we coast through nature's glorious labyrinth

By Ohio we are bleary and starting to unravel
Charles scours the Interstate for a place to crash
For three hours, all we see are no vacancy signs
Every motel is spilling over with refugees like us

He stops in the back of a huge truck stop
The highway ships are circling, waiting to dock
The band settles in to sleep wherever they may fall
I take my sleeping bag to the edge of the cornfield
And find a row where the light can't find me
And fall asleep in the rustle of silk and stalks

When I awake the next morning I have to laugh
One night I have a spot on National Television
And a bed with starched sheets in a posh uptown hotel
And the next night I'm sleeping in an Ohio cornfield
With frost forming on the dirt in my hair

We drive through the sweet Kentucky forest
Through groves of hickory, ash and pine
Out to the distillery past the village of Clermont
Where whiskey has been made night and day
For longer than anyone can remember

I meet the relatives of old Jim Beam
And notice the red noses of the whole family
And they lead me into a place with a thousand people
To play them songs that I always carry with me
Under a huge tent full of whiskey drinkers
And after the music come piles of meat
And after the meat come bottles of whiskey

And a drawing to see which employee might win
The Grand Prize of a brand new Harley Davidson

Everyone tries to focus on his or her ticket stub number
As the lesser prizes are handed out one by one
And when they call out the Grand Prize winner
There is a murmur that ripples through the crowd
As if a rather large boulder had been dropped into a lake

The rumble turned to disbelief as the attention turned
To a large black woman and her whole family running
And screaming with abandon across the floor to the podium
Where the presenters looked back and forth to each other
As if to ask each other how this could have happened
The lady, wild with animated glee, sat on the Harley
And revved the engine and blew kisses to the dumbfounded
Whiskey drinkers who shook their heads in disbelief
As the woman's husband took over the driver's seat
They had tears in their eyes, and they held each other tightly
And cruised the Harley Davidson out into the cool night
Down the road to Old Clermont
Under moonlit Hickory, Ash and Pine.

After leaving Kentucky the road kept winding
And in my journal I tried to keep up
We detoured back through Texas
And spun a loop and were hurled up to the Midwest
Chicago, Minneapolis and Kansas City
After a figure eight back thru Dallas
We rubberbanded back to the East and Down South

We then coasted back to the Texas Hill country
Combed the wind out of our hair
Did our laundry, had a plate of enchiladas
Then packed for part two of the Tour de la Trip

We mirrored what we had done already
Went from San Diego to Seattle and Salt Lake City

Down through Colorado and beautiful Santa Fe
I would tell you all the details
As I have told you before, I wrote it in my book
But the airplane people lost my guitars
And with them my journals gone with the wind

And so we came in for a crash landing
Back where we began, dear ol' Texas
To hibernate though December and January
To Heal our Wounds, Patch our Gear
And to play a New Years Eve show so weird
That I can safely breathe easy, there will never be another
    like it.

And now we rest up and save ourselves for Italy
I buy a stack of paper and get film for my brain
We must live it as it comes, catch it as it passes
The road goes on forever but we'll never be the same again

LAREDO EURO

Isabella must have been Columbus's Mistress,
Columbus crossed her ocean
At the crackle of her skirt
From Spain, he brought Silver Trinkets,
Moroccan Horses, Christian Dogma
And a ship full of Rare Euro Diseases,

And returned to Spain
With Golden Trinkets, Rare Jungle Diseases
And Cuban Cigars for Queen Isabella
Columbus had a weakness for the island girls
They writhed through his battered sailor dreams
Like dolphins in a moonlit lagoon
Lips painted with the juice of wild berries
Extremities bound in Bracelets de Oro

The Queen who propels my journeys,
Unlike Columbus

Is she who lives in the Whirlwind Of Music
And only comes out
When the sun has closed Her prying eyes
Once again I have crossed the Atlantic at night
And sentenced myself to 30 days
Touring the Old Country
To see old friends, play one-night stands
And to stock my Cabinets with Ancestral Memorie

Being from a young Texas town
Grants a man a unique perspective
We can look out as if we are within a television set
To compare the Ancient with the Instant
And seeing how well the Ancient has held up
Makes us hungry for TV dinners

We land in Milano with a bang and a gulp
And rub the cornflakes from our eyes
We sleepwalk from the plane with fellow zombies
To Il Grande Salon d'il Luggage Snake
Only to find, after double-checking with the proper authorities
That Jesse's suitcase and mine are both missing
The Baroness of Luggage Lost reassures us repeatedly
That our luggage might possibly, someday, be found . . .

I wave to the Customs Police
Who stroke their sleek machine guns,
French-inhale unfiltered Gauloises,
And pet their German Shepherds . . .
Since I have no bags
I obviously have nothing to declare
And do so cynically with disgust . . .

Waiting just beyond the International Glass
Are the smiling faces of the Flying Carlinis
Who prime us with coffee, good cheer, and croissants
And invite us to lunch at their casa in Sesto
We sit at the table in a kind of humble reverence
And a great calm descends upon our Depressurized Souls

Bowls of Spaghetti, bottles of Red Wine,
Bread and Cheese from the barrels of Parma

What an Art the Italians have made of The Meal,
Centered their social, sexual and political lives around it
They argue and reconcile in the same meal
And eat course after course,
Stretching the event to hours or more
Yet are not fat, lazy or slovenly
But are always late to work or to meet their lovers
So they drive 140 miles an hour to apologize
And invite the offended party to a meal once again . . .

But even the Eternal Faucet of God's Cappuccino
Cannot waylay the inevitable Lag
That conquers our dying wakefulness
So off we go to check in to our Digs

After a small sleep injection at the Parc Hotel
The Carlinis call on us for dinner on the Piazza

And once again we remember that the real charm of Italy
Is the grace with which people enjoy their lives
Their inherited passion is with family and friends
Never do I witness insulting distractions waged on the
    moment
Such as a radio or TV on during dinner
All family events are played out together,
In the common arena of the dining room
Where generations decide what's future and what's history . . .

The first stop is Vicenza where a large meal awaits
And we wonder if we have been dropped into heaven
After months on the highways of America
Eating in hostile truckstops and junkstops
We imagine that we have landed in paradise
A Heaven that smells of garlic and wine
And baking bread and fresh-cut flowers

The Music we make seems to pour itself
So fortunate are we to be vessels
Effortlessly as well does the crowd accept
What we have no idea what we're giving
And to show their gratitude they storm the dressing room
Which I leave to the others surrounded

After a performance I am most vulnerable
And so have a desperate need for solitude
Ironically this is the time the audience is most animated
And desire to express their emotion up close and in person
After a few breaths and a shirt change
I go out to meet my wonderful Italian friends
To accept their appreciation,
To try and understand their crazy conversation,
And to look into the eyes of their mysterious women . . .

Within minutes of dozing off
I am awakened by a flutter of bats in my bowels

I open my eyes to a room strung in gauze
With the light pouring pale yellow paint down the wall
There is a huge Vulture in my belly
It lunges for my throat the minute I rise
It stretches its neck to the light inside my mouth
I hold on to the bed rails as the room rocks violently
I imagine I have been poisoned and will soon explode
Never such Nausea has my body experienced
The exception being Paris after a late night Wimpy Burger
I now remember crawling up the subway stairs
On all fours down the street begging for help
I barely remember the face of the kind old gentleman
Who called for me an ambulance
And the doctor who ordered me to eat
A four-course dinner and a full bottle of Beaujolais
And the beautiful nurse who fed me gently . . .

I toss and turn till the morning light
Thinking it will go away or else I'll die
The phone rings with Paulo asking if I am ready to travel

I ask her to call me a doctor and let the band travel on
This she does as the minutes crawl like hours
The doctor comes and tells me to eat a good meal
And to always drink wine with my meals, not water

We take a taxi to the dizzy, ancient train yard
The interior rocks like a ship on high seas
I hover around *il bano*, feeling faint and pale
Searching in vain for the strength to board
The motion of the train actually settles my head
And the sunny countryside is a welcome sight
I slip in and out of my blurry, dim body
I must rise above, no Rescue Squadron in sight

The train stops only seconds in Sesto
We literally leap from the platform as it takes off
My healing leg takes a jolt, transferring my focus
The Mercedes taxi takes us, slowly pleeze,
To the Hotel Parc where I doze
Waking at play time, still queasy . . .
Minutes before we walk on stage
I'm in The John throwing up like mad
I remember little about the night
Except how good it felt to sweat
In the hot stage lights
And the sea of friendly faces
Responding in rhythm to the beat
And how brilliantly Teye and Jesse played together
And how Davis and Glenn propped me up
Feeling that I may evaporate at any second
Into a quick sizzle and a puff of grey steam
Then realizing I made it,
Unbelievably, through the night
Finishing the set triumphantly,
Even doing an encore
And going even later to the billiard parlor
To be filmed by Italian TV
Playing "Cinque Birrelli" with the Maestro of Italy

I force down amber pasta and a glass of vino,
The food falls forever like a bucket down a dry well
I sleep that night as if I had been shot in the head
And dream of the Moroccan desert
And the purity of emptiness . . .

I walk in the morn by lake Maggiore
To the village of Sesto
Noticing a turquoise boat
Sunk under 3 feet of water by the shore
Silver fish swim around the stern,
Not noticing my gaze
Suddenly I think of the lovers
In the cafe on the Isle in the middle of the lake
From my last visit here, a little over a year ago
Suddenly becoming sad
At my worldly loneliness
I had just given away a love
And confessed it all to Alejandro
Still Sharon and Marie wait for my calls each night
But I can never tell them the real sadness in my heart
I try to sound as if all is rosy, but they hear my anguish
And ask if something has gone wrong
I confess that I have been pierced by arrows
But not to worry, each arrow is a song
And songs are soon
Left haunting the streets like ghosts

We have a few days to heal
And the rain seems to help
Teije travels to Rome,
He's new to this kind of living
Davis writes postcards to his hundred cousins
And runs up his phone bill
Charles and Glenn buy Lombardy wine
From the man on the corner
Who has a lake running under his shop
And an actress for a wife

Who nags at his every sentence
Jesse sleeps and reads, and drinks,
Then reads and sleeps, and drinks
Time slows to a crawl; a cold rain sets in,
Misting the lake in grey
There are no distractions nearby
No TV, no nothin'
Just the ancient pace of Italy,
Passionate conversation out the window
The smell of Bread, Garlic, Grappa
And simmering tomatoes
Creeping up the granite stairs in dim light
On ancient footprints
By the third day we are ready to roll,
Rigor mortis has set in
So it's over the mountains we sail,
Ready for anything
Thru snaky black tunnels that curved like bowels
Tossing us back into the sunlight
Before devouring us again
Bright yellow cubes of stucco cling to the sides of cliffs by
    the sea
As if built by humongous architectural hornets
A feeling is triggered in me that we are entering a nest
That the busy little Fiats are red ants, the busses, caterpillars,
And we are a visiting party of insects entering the work camp
To either be welcomed by the home boys or devoured at the
    gate
And our bones tossed in the sea like so much flotsam

Alex, our driver, begins to show his true personality,
He has an ability to become so lost
That even he cannot believe he is lost
He would say, "I am notta losta,
I justa don'ta knowa where I ama. . ."
Even after stopping to ask directions he would say,
"How can they a knowa where to senda me,"
"If they have a notta been a there them a selves a . . ."
As we peruse the Genoan streets

Analyzing un-logical possibilities
Having not a clue, myself,
As all streets fracture like wagon spokes
But using this opportunity to see the city
With fresh and different eyes
The strange mixture of Ancient Beauty
With hideous Post War Modern
Concrete structures designed by lobotomized architects
Connected by Fascist trained mechanical engineers
Who cared only to get from here to there
Concerned not that the people who traveled their structures
Might actually want to enjoy the space in-between their
    destinations
As did the people of old, when architecture was in harmony
With the earth and the culture of those who contributed to it

Ahh, but the beauties of Genoa far outweigh her flaws
As we found upon digging deeper into her mysteries
The curved golden buildings framing the busy coast
The harbor of vessels from the Absolute Mediterranean
Bobbing only slightly as if too proud to bob
Gleaming in the sun against a backdrop of red tile, painted
    mud,
Sculpture of white fake masts rigged with astro-cable
Causing my head to swim in speculation
And contemplation of the Modern Italian Mind
And why my Texas music, so foreign to the roots of this
    culture
Has been absorbed into its fabric, thus affecting my life, my
    family
And my amigos present and future
Not to mention altering my course and destination
Till the Saints go Marchin' In and the Cows Come Home,
    whew . . .

The Teatro Albatros was filled with Spanish eyes
And the passion of the dance rivaled that of suicide lovers

Each cannot live without the other, yet each suffocates the
    other
And begins a cycle that can only end in catastrophe . . .
Or if both lovers survive, they learn the ultimate paradox
That to love is to set free, like the sparrow from the cage
Like the wolf from the chain, so that each spirit may soar
Above the bounds of jealous love, freely and independently
So that each may find the purpose of their lives, be lonely as hell,
And drink the euphonious wine of forgetfulness
Till they wake in the gilded gutter of understanding . . .

Here they come again, sure as rain, them dreaded Spanish
    Blues
The Flamenco Maestro is once again head down,
His hands over both sides of his temples
His every movement that of depression,
Striking fear into all those in his vicinity
I become furious that he controls people that way
And lash out with a hyena like cackle
Teye throws his flamenco hat across the hotel lobby
And groans in Spanish agony
I semi-expect a tall dark gypsy woman

In a black lace dress and a veil
To burst into the lobby wailing in tears
Suddenly ripping a burst of thirty-second notes
With the heels of her shabby satin pumps
They ricochet against the fake brick linoleum
Like machine-gun fire in an Andalusia gymnasium
As candles are lit and prayers are whispered
Then I expect a one-eyed gaucho with a pencil mustache
To steal up behind her dagger in hand
Then El Maestro, as if he heard the Bells of St. Toledo,
Would lift his tortured head
And reach for his weeping Reyes guitar
Like all great martyrs, he would right the situation
With merely a flick of his wrist
The most dissonant of all Spanish chords
Would emanate from his Guitar and the Evil Gaucho
Would be overtaken with lunacy
Slitting his own throat and dropping with his cape
Billowing into a heap onto the hotel lobby floor
Teye would not even acknowledge
The standing ovation he gets from the registered guests
Nor pay the least bit of attention to the dancing maiden
Bestowing him with a flutter of passionate kisses
He only, silently, lays his head back on the table
And reaches for his tortured temples . . .

I went to my room and dreamed
Of beautiful young lusty Italian Angels
Like the kind Botticelli painted late at night
When the scent of Wild Narcissus
Blew through his upstairs window
Causing his Candle to flicker,
Making the Wings in his paintings
Appear to flutter in the dark spaces
Giving him an Erection
Only Venus could restrain
She simply closed up her shell
And let Helli-Celli sleep it off
Face down in his palette of ochres, alizarins, and cobalts . . .

I awake the next morning, groggy from dreams
Not wanting the wheels to roll or the earth to turn
Or the ocean to recede or the wind to howl
Dreading the clatter of engine parts, Sparkplug Fire
The whine of wheels and Rude Road Rock
Only wanting the dreams to linger
And the cold sheets to cocoon my naked body
But when a telephone ring stabbed my consciousness
Grudgingly conceded to motion
Throwing clothes across the room
To the general vicinity of my open luggage
After a quick check under the bed and in the bath
Grabbing the suitcase by the nape of the neck
And dragging it like an unclaimed corpse
Down 6 flights of sharp slick stairs
To the hotel's dark and crumbling coffee shop
For a double shot of rocket fuel
And a sugar coated tiger's paw
And out into the diesel morning
Crawling with sawed-off delivery vans,
Shopping women with shawls on their heads
And red eyed musicians with snakes in their hair
Looking at their Fiat van
As if it were a four wheeled, sheet metal torture chamber
Revved up to drag them against their will
Four hundred kilometers to the east
To be paroled for the night
Pardoned to Perform, in sweet Ferrara,
Where it becomes clear as Grappa
Why we are chained to the highway,
Why the highways are chained to the earth
And why the earth is locked
In the chains of the relentless universe . . .

LETTER TO LAREDO — EUROPE
February through March 1996

ON THE RUN AGAIN

What would *you* do if your days were numbered?
Check yourself in to the Nightmare Factory?
And Count the ticking of your days
On grave faces of infirmary computers?

Fling Yourself from the highway bridge?
To make damn sure to shorten the Clock even more?
Would you Make a pilgrimage to the Holy Land
To dodge Sanctified Bullets from the Guns of the Holy?

Or would you, if you could, return to the Road
To comb vast spaces across Mother America
While making Music with lifelong friends
In the cities between those spaces?

Would you seek Refuge in Harmony?
And Share in Song, withholding nothing?
Would you give everything that you could give
And stand Firm in the Floodlight holding back tears?

Not guided by logic, not determined by reason
Passion drives my waking moments, I dodge evil Panic
I toss to the Ether my Circle of Breaths
And I fear for Beloved Survivors

For fifty some odd years I've walked the walk
Of the prisoner whose fate is sealed
Knowingly, I've teased the Hooded Rider, the Ego and the Id
By staying one roll ahead of the Sickle

Imagine forty thousand pounds of Hurtling Steel
Navigating a gauntlet of equally Heavy Missiles
Eighty miles an hour through the bloodshot night

Waiting on the Dawn to decide Morning's fate

Day after day and night after night
Grown men bouncing around the walls of a bus
Driven by spirits to deliver their Muse
Then feeling back through the dark for the Exit Road.

We depart in Celebration at One in the morning
Wives and Families dancing trunk to bus
Dogs barking, cars circling, kissing tearful farewells
Amid the idling smell of headlights and diesel

With the hiss of airbrakes, a new tour extends
With the Driver scanning for Magnetic West
Through Stonewall and Junction, Ozona and Iraan
Where Dry meets Parched under the Arid Moon

We sleep in suspension like jelly in a bowl
And dream pitched snippets of snapshots and flashes
We ram through the dark in faith held blind
Stopping only for fuel and divine inspiration

I'm shaken in Alpine by the Marathon Sun
I rise to walk in the cool dry morn
An occasional pickup, an Explorer or a Ram
Drives at a crawl to make the long day longer

Descendants of The Apache and the Chickenshit Coronado
Take turns at the pump as desert dwellers must
They turn slowly as the Rancher, the latest badlands Honcho
Daunts them all with his Megaton Black Silverado

After dinner with Amigos we cross the Tracks
To the Church on the hill by the concrete lot
Lured by accordions and a driving Bajo
Only to find a Hooded DJ with a blown PA

We glide on two wheels, Jimmie Dale and I
Through the quiet mountain town unmoved by TV
Danger emerges, we hear shots ring out
We retreat to so-called safety of the Known

By noon the next day we're in the city of Tucson
By Hotel Congress on the railroad tracks
The trains whistle blows as the Circus starts to load
I'm taken back to the years of my Gypsy life.

Shadows in the dark keep a watch on us
We're too visible to hide from what we can't see
They steal my green bike in the white daylight
Chained to a pole, two feet from door

Adios poor Tucson you've seen better days
There once was a time when I loved you
If I make it across the desert I'll kiss the sea
And send seashells back to your thieves, *Cash On Delivery*

Our picture is in the paper on Sunset Blvd
It startles us to the point of laughter
Butch reminds us, Mirrors don't remember Reflections
Jimmie adds, Whatever Reflects is but Illusion

Hollywood is the Black Hole Center of the World
A Gravitational Vortex that constantly consumes
All energies drawn into its Realm of Influence
Just to Survive another night on the Town

We see old friend Ventura from a café window
And take it as a sign that Everything is Alright
Thirty years ago, we met in the 14th street house
As mutual explorers in pursuit of a Map

The show was passable, neither inspired nor shabby
The crowd roared, unexpectedly, for more

My Patagonia amigos roared in the back room
And then we all roared to Boardner's together

I walked for miles down San Juan Capistrano
And bought a bike from a Surfer on Crank
I rode away in glee, replenished and whole
As the tops of the palms floated through the clouds

At the Coach House onstage the muse has relaxed
We fall in to a beat and then set it free
Sometimes a Room is in harmony with itself
If only that could happen in the World . . .

The hills of Marin beg for the Eye
To follow their lithe, alluring curves
We coast forever past Strawberry Fields
To the Wild Anise Lake where the ducks quacked our names

Angela and Bob tell stories at lunch
Of the history of the Nicasio Ranchers
And the Spanish school they helped to build
To protect the Culture for Tomorrow

The Hippies came down with a new generation
To celebrate the Fourth of July
We shared the changes that have fallen upon our planet
And belted out the Chorus in spite of Ourselves

My bicycle and I huffed our way to the Coit Tower
Then flew like a hawk down hill to the pier
Where Market meets Bridge at the Docks of the Bay
On to The Phoenix to meet Marie and Sharon

San Francisco flopped from poor to rich
And flipped just as quick from rich back to poor
Like musicians who go from feast to famine
When Songs are less popular than Ideas

I get word Joe Strummer's in town
Although our shows are on the same day
We swap notes through Mark and Wendell
But, alas, we must Roll in different directions in the night

Santa Cruz is a song who is losing its melody
Armed raiders now command her streets
But the Rio was a shelter from the gangster's storm
And the audience had a front row seat

So it's on to the Fair, up on Marin so High
Where the Prosperous come to spin the wheel
Seven shades of Khaki, five Grays and a White
Tone down the brash colors of Confusion

The fireworks were mirrored from a man-made lake
With a musical theme, Patriotic War
The red fireballs received the most Primal Response
As if sanctioned and approved by Rush Limbaugh

So it's back to the Bus, the Mother of Travel
A thousand miles of bumps between us and Sweet Boulder
I open Red Wine as a Cushion for the Road
And Brace Body and Brain for the brutality ahead

I peek out the window at the crack of Morning
And see Vast Salt Nothingness framed by Neon Casino
The summer sun, remorseless, after breakfast with Losers
I ride to the Salt Flats for lunch with Chinese

Casinos are the graveyard for any True Gambler
They're a pit and a Piss Hole for Corporate Death
I shouldn't be so harsh, but I'd rather be flailin'
A Hubcap for a banjo on a windy Irish Do

Tommy won a Bundle but I think he was lyin'
Nobody wins when the Odds are Uneven

Life is supported by camaraderie and water
None of which matters in the Desert

The Indians gather far from Flim Flam Town
And swap Stories in front of the Mega Wholesale Store
As Traders, they were robbed of their license to trade
As Soothsayers, lost the need to conform

So it's adios, forever, to Windover Nevada
I'll not miss you for a moment or a thousand years
As we cross the Alien Salt Flats and Wild Rolling Wyoming
To the city of mystical Boulder in the shadow of the Crown

I glide through the streets on my two wheel machine
Happy like a sailor to be back on Still Earth
I live for the times I have Wind in my face
And Pray Thanks that my soul breathes Music

A day off in Kansas City looking for Frank Lloyd Wright
A dusk with the boys in Whoopee Thai Heaven
We churn on to Nashville for a Romp on the River
Then to close down The Sunset with Heather and the Boys

I had not been to Chattanooga since old runnin' days
In fact the only thing I recognized was the Pool Hall
Each Memory I have painted, in part, by State of Mind
Has no essential obligation to the Others

Ring around Atlanta, Lord, I'm down on Peachtree Lane
Where the Dot Com Geeks meet the Good Ol' Boys
And the Work Camp Girls meet the Media Types
And slug gin to the Blues of the Lost Southern Myth

We met newspaper reporters backstage at Chastain
And told Stories we were now beginning to disbelieve
Then jammed by the dock with Keb' Mo' and friends
With songs passed down from more believable Times

I wake in the parking lot where Ponce de Leon
Abandoned his quest for the Fountain of Youth
Bruised and Hung over from his bouts with the Natives
He just wanted coffee, a croissant and a smoke

Like Ponce de Leon, I, too, have a Vision
Not nearly as Vain, but equally Outlandish

I believe Love can solve all the questions
Of those who think The Answer has vanished

The South is a quagmire of Notions and Feelings
Thought to have been Lost but then Reappear
Disguised only slightly by gesture and Accent
Familiar as Family and welcome as Rain

In city after city there Seems to be Magic
As friends from lost times appear from the Mist
If only this Era could be rewound
To make room for the Timeless, to spend more Time

The Bus smells home as it crisscrosses I-10
As we're slammed by potholes, Swamp Road Inertia
Bodies reeling like bowls of angry oil
Reaching for an Anchor but finding Thin Air

The Boys are suffering from sailor's disease
The hours drag by, and the Play gets Rough
Jimmie locked Rob inside the 3 × 3 Pisser
Rob crashed out the window, in reply

I awake in a Louisiana glass repair shop
And walk a mile through a Battlezone to a get a bite to eat
On to New Orleans to the House of Blues
As the night gets sweeter and ends with a Bang

It's good to see Gatemouth, He has the soul of an Angel
We talk about Stubb and his Holy Kitchen
In Reverence to the Memory of that which is Mighty
Gate speaks from the Heart, he don't mince nothin'

Another long Haul to Wichita Falls
With Jimmie's uncle telling stories of yesteryear

A common thread, the dust bowl days, connects the tales
Of those who survived, only the Strong stay Alive

We're home by morning, for twenty measly hours
My girls come to meet me, faces flush with Love
Thirty days I've been gone, it seems like a Year
No time to re-charge, just Savor the Moment

We join the troupe of Bluegrass Stars
Tossed in the pit without a Cue
Ralph Stanley, the Whites, Ms Krause and All
Down from the Mountain, and Up Against the Wall

We bounce off of Dallas and rebound Home
With a week to catch up on bills and Sleep
Walks in the woods and sashaying through the Trees
Fills me with Heaven and draws away the Tears

The TV is Rabid with Drums of War
George Dubya Bush is Stuck on Revenge
Survival, in *his* mind, depends on Aggression
Mesmerized by Destruction, slinging Power like Mud

The Networks have become the Puppets of the government
Smiling, showing teeth, from the sides of their Mouths
The Winner is the channel that Hurls the most Dazzle
With Competing *ALERTS!* and graphics that *Swirl*

Green night war burning white holes in TV's phosphor
War planes dropping World's biggest bombs
On the mud streets of struggling Baghdad
Blowing to dust all Innocent who stray into Danger

Sanctified and Justified by *Military Intelligence*
Innocent death Justified by *Collateral Damage*
Angry, proud farmers renamed *Insurgents*
And they who are not Christian are deemed *Militant!!!*

When the TV is dark does The Madness cease?
Talk of War is contagious like the Talk of Peace.
"Weapons of Mass Destruction" is the phrase of the day
Why not suggest "Gardens of Mass Creation"?

I hear the Honk of the Big Red Bus by the oak tree
The diesel, sub sonic, churning up clouds of July Dust
The dogs climb over each other to greet the enormous Intruder
Barking wildly, running head down, without fear

The Band arrives as usual, half early and half late
Each man mapping his miniscule rectangle of real estate
Preparing for another fifteen thousand miles of road
To Points unknown, Spaces unseen

Sharon and Marie help pack my Gear
And load us down with blankets and apples
The dogs run through the isles, sniffing for clues
As to where we have been and what might be to eat

I close my eyes and shake off the Dread
I don't want to leave the paradise we've made
The Trees agree, they sway my way
With windy scent of Agarita and Wisteria

Once again we're off, down Highway 71
It's 3 A.M. and the land is dark
The rocking of the road puts us all to sleep
To dream the dreams of Sailors out to Sea

The smell of Tortillas wafts us awake
In Lubbock on the plains by the Taco Village
Then on to Amarillo and a stop to sleep
For Fred the Driver to store his resources

I turned my motel room into a recording studio
With Balanced mattresses parallel to the walls

And pillows and cushions to soften the Angles
That the sound might have less far to Travel

Two songs I captured before the couple next door
Commenced on a drunken, bloody free-for-all
Screaming at each Other, attempting in Vain
To convince the other their own alter egos were Right.

It seems everyone would rather be Right than Real
But the Action bogs down when Understanding is highest
Truth has no Charisma when viewed on TV
Commercials must be sold for Survival On Air.

Selling begets restraints, birthing Commercial Truth
Non-stop deception, government biased perception
Selling Sensationalism, leaning on the lurid
Hoodwinking the Drooling Shills, to insure Major Network
    Profit

Reality TV, an oxymoron of the highest degree
Is in competition with Cable News and the Crocodile Hunter
For the "Blatant Imprudence" Award of the Century
To be presented at the Season Finale of "American Idol"

I ride my bike to see Carthel and Gwen
My only Uncle and Aunt left in the world
We sat in the living room on the couch
And sweetly talked of dogs and cats for an hour

So it's sayonara to Amarillo as the bus rolls at midnight
We climb all night up the Incline of the Plains
In sleep I dream of old sad Raton
Weaving up the pass to golden Trinidad

A mile above the ocean in the Vortex of the Country
I awake in Thunder to the sound of mad Denver
My bike has a flat, miles to the Station
But I'll sweat uphill to coast down the Wind

Alas, the sweet Denver of the Beats is Long Gone
Its City Council, like Austin's, decreed Enchantment taboo.
Where the Public forsake Art, and bowed, instead, to Cash
And Sold Community Faith to the Corporate Promise

I ride for hours through changing downtown
Where striking glass buildings reflect stone from the past
Where the Pace of Commerce pushes all else aside
And the Dreamers have all moved to Utah

We depart out of Denver to the Crys of Sirens
Soon Wyoming blows its sweet night air
Through our dreams of the Western Vast Wide Open
And awake to a new day in the City of the Mormon

Up the hill to the Capitol perched upon a Bluff
High above the desert floor
Where Rulers view their Subjects and the Great Salt Lake
From Halls of Marble where ring the Echoes of Law

We coast back by the Temple and the Garden Walls
We feel the Rumble of the Organ Vibrate our Spine
Through the wide streets, Devotees with Cameras
Scour the tidy streets for a Holy Graven Image

After dinner we cruise Restless and Unbound
To the old train station abandoned but strong
An Invisible Chain across a Simulated Street
Stops Butch and any perceived forward progress

Upon returning Jimmie describes a similar parable:
When an Irresistible Force meets an Unmovable Object
What could possibly be the outcome?
And then the answer: An Unimaginable Event . . .

We play downtown in the Galivan Center
And hit our stride about Midway
to Performer in sync with the Unprepared Perceivers
In a Dance with the Harmony of the Spheres

It is 800 Miles to Santa Fe
And Sixteen Long Hours to Do It
Fred hunkers down, focused and ready
To cross Utah, Wyoming, Colorado and Nuevo Mexico

Our Santa Fe Amigos showed up for show
And partook of our Salsa and shared our Sweet Wine
How good to see Friends after Time has softened
The Differences that we once deemed awkward

The road to Las Vegas was used by the Spanish
As a Pass to the West and the Cities of Gold
At Imus's Ranch, the Dying Children danced
To "Wavin' My Heart Goodbye," with glee . . .

The Cameras panned around the Room
And saw only that which was Visible
That is the Trouble with the world of Objects
Only Seers can see Inside the Light

We edge away to our next destination
Past the Western Town painted in Corporate Logos
And Wave to Faces we will never again see
Through the dust that soon covers our tracks

A Mansion in Heaven is a worthwhile objective
Some want it Now, in this Sad ol' World
With Worldly Riches comes an Ironic Bonus,
The Hell-hounds that stalk Influence and Cash

Northward to Taos climbs the Big Red Bus
While the band makes a game of the Excitement
National TV in the morning, then playing again that night
At the request of the Most Famous Person in the World

Of course, Celebrity, like Life, is relative and brief
Although no one denies the power of Presence
When a Movie Star invades the Emotions of the Viewer
And resides in the character forever

Julia greets us with Charm and Grace
I introduce her to Sharon, Jimmie and Butch
She is glad to see Joel and bids us Welcome
As she has graciously done twice before

The distant mountains are soft like cotton
As the afternoon light spins veils of gold
The music drifts softly across the cool green field
To the tent beneath the Starry, Starry Night

The band Fires Up and the dark begins to Spin
The Blood begins to Boil and it pumps up the Wind
The Lungs commence to Pound and the Dance it does Begin
The colors start to Blur and the muscles start to bend . . .

By the End of the night, even the Band is dancing
Around a Mexican Hat in the middle of the floor
Crazy with Abandon and Midnight Majic
Parting ways with Loved Ones and on to the bus

We laugh through the mountains and on to the Plain
Where one by one we drift into road sleep
In the morning I awake in a Wal-Mart parking lot
Between a ditch and a Dairy Queen Motel 8

I laugh again at the irony of it all
On a Movie Star's Estate the night before
In a Kansas parking lot the next morning
Taking Inventory of an Intangible Existence

I make tea and write for six hours
Trying to Extract the Truth from the Inventory
In the End I decided that it was too much to Face
So got lost in Wal-Mart exploring Chinese trinkets

The next week we spend Racking Up the miles
Columbia to Madison, Chicago to West Virginia

Insides smashed against skin's bruised Boundary
America's highway budget squander'd on silly bombs

Once again, America fights an Invisible Foe
A word, an Idea that has no idea of what it Is
The enemy is Faceless, without an Army or a Name
An enemy who has no country, cannot be bombed into bits.

The military always suggest Force over Understanding
With no Concern over Damage Done
Blind Fools, don't they know that War breeds War?
That the Offspring of the Dead breed a new brand of Hate?

The road breeds potholes, I'm losing my mind
That is, until I realize I have no mind to lose
I Travel Inside and find the Place
Where Everything and Nothing Harmonize

In Circular Breath my weariness does vanish
Dissolving into Waves that rise and fall
With the Boundless Sea in a sphere of blue
Floating in Time through a Universe of Space . . .

West Virginia was a hoot in a hot-ass barn
And the Band were all characters in a petrified play
Like a hillbilly still-life dreamed-up by Dali
Down-home as Cornbread and Surreal as Steam

What has six balls and fucks rednecks?
The West Virginia State Lottery . . .
Robbie relates this joke via cell phone
In four seconds, and a breath, from a thousand miles away

Humor, it saves us, repeatedly
We marvel at the Absurd, unpredictable and random
That which might be Misery for non-travelers,
Becomes inevitable for those on the move

Back on the bus we weave the mountains
And seek out the Potomac and the Capitol City
Land of Laws and Looney Legislation
Where the world is played like a chess game

Enron and Worldcom enter the conversation
With how Big Money helped elect the Inner Hunkies
Nothing new, Power hides behind Banks and Oil
Concealed by Mirrors, Lawyers and Junkies

The populace of the bus jumps into the banter
As the Topic of the Hour floats without help
"They passed a new law of averages" said Butch from the blue
"But it failed to impress the old school of lawyers"

All of the News that runs off of The Hill
Has taken a noticeable, Surreal Complexion
Logic Itself has turned Anal and Rude
Supported by Legions men in Blue Suits

Then suddenly, just as quick as it did arise,
We left Reason behind and moved to the Mystic
The world of Matter will never make sense
For those who seek Devine Emptiness

How blessed we are to have the luxury to rejoice
Among friends in the camaraderie of the moment
To howl freely without restraint down the road to nowhere
Unbound by ambition, but Bound for Glory

If, someday, someone asks, what I did with my life
I'll look them in the eye and laugh out loud
I'll ask if they, have ever studied the Heavens
To wonder beyond this Quagmire Planet?

What were you doing 18 billion years ago?
When we were all One Atom, bigger than Little Rock?
Did you breathe? How did you Prepare?
For a Bang so Big that it flipped your Ass double

Inside Out, a Human Möbius Strip made of flesh
Figure 8 shaped, Asshole in the Center
A Black Hole for the Anti-Matter Crowd
Providing a shape for the Cosmos to Ponder

How did you hitch your scatter'd Elements?
To a burning Earth plopped from the Sun?
How did you survive the Comet Crash that filled the Seas?
After crawling ashore to breathe Earth's flammable
   atmosphere?

When did Consciousness slap you Awake?
And toss you a Mirror and a tank of Laughing Gas
Did it leave you on the beach, peering between Stars?
Looking back in Time for a Measly Clue . . .

FLATLANDERS TOUR
Summer 2002

AFTERWORD

These journals were written on the road, in the wind, against gravity and inertia, in the moment, on the move, in darkness and in light, from song to song, from road to road, on expeditions impossible, for no reason, not expecting to be read, for their own sake, and, perhaps selfishly, for the sake of the sanity of the writer.

Some of these passages began as notes for future songs; some as riddles to solve in the meantime; some, snapshots of what was flying by, just out of reach, so to savor at a later date when the wheels stopped rolling, and the gears quit grinding and the engines shut down . . .

They were written in pencil and ballpoint, in Sharpie and ink pen. They were written on grocery bags, on yesterday's paper, on café napkins and on the palms of my hands, up one finger and down the other. They were scratched on windowsills, and on the bottoms of drawers inside hotel dressers. Some were written in freight trains; some in limousines. They were jotted down on streetcars and on subways, on bicycles, airplanes and ferries. Some, I dreamed and some dreamed me.

So many pieces were lost along the way; four years drove away from the Chelsea Hotel in the trunk of a Yellow Cab never to return; another year was gone when I woke to a swollen Texas river rising in my motel room; other sections were left behind in haste or abandoned by choice. The miracle is how many of the pieces made it through.

Some of these songs had to be translated, by myself, not rec-
ognizing the intent of the speaker. Sentences, lost in a fold, had
to be added; some, found in broad daylight, asked to be re-direct-
ed. One canto, hacked in the dark on a Radio Shack computer
coming into potholed Chicago at midnight, was so full of mis-
struck keys that they became part of the song's personality.

This book is dedicated to those with whom I have shared my
journey. Whether they be loved ones, band mates, spiritual
chaperones or road crew, these stories would not have been the
same without their presence. And to those who have made this
expedition possible, I want to thank them for their patience and
understanding. Otherwise, we might never have left the station.

It is not the nature of the gypsy to look in the rear view mirror. Now and then he might sneak a peek to check for the presence of a cloaked skeleton, riding a flat-black Harley, wielding
a silver scythe. Not that it matters. The code of the West is still
the same; stay in the present with one eye open, know your
water holes, and give the Grim Reaper a run for his money.

Future bards might not be required to travel in the physical
world. They may cross borders wirelessly in the virtual domain
and navigate oceans with a roll of an eye. But there will always
be those who want to venture beyond the horizon just to see
what is there . . . To those, I hope these accounts will give a
glint of inspiration . . .